# Between Worlds

# BETWEEN WORLDS

## SOR JUANA ON CULTURE, GENDER, AND THE DESIRE FOR KNOWLEDGE

Richard Frontjes

Political Animal Press
Toronto • Chicago

Political Animal Press
www.politicalanimalpress.com

Distributed by the University of Toronto Press

Library and Archives Canada Cataloguing in Publication

Frontjes, Richard, 1972-, author
Between worlds : Sor Juana on culture, gender, and the desire for knowledge / Richard Frontjes.

Includes bibliographical references.
Issued in print and electronic formats.
ISBN 978-1-895131-31-4 (softcover).--ISBN 978-1-895131-34-5 (PDF)

1. Juana Inés de la Cruz, Sister, 1651-1695--Criticism and interpretation. I. Title.

PQ7296.J6Z58 2018 861'.3 C2018-905262-7
C2018-905263-5

Cover design and illustration by Ingrid Paulson
Printed and bound in Canada

For my family

# CONTENTS

# Preface: Navigating Cultural Encounter with Sor Juana

In April of the year 2000, I wandered into Ros's Cabinet Shop in Romeo, Michigan, looking for work. I was prepared to turn around and walk right out again—I'd been through enough applications to know that most floundered. Instead, however, they handed me a cotton rag and some lacquer thinner: I was hired.

I'd been bouncing from job to job for about six weeks when I stumbled into the shop, and I assumed that cleaning gluey overspray off Formica would likewise be short-lived. I'd been a trainee for the 2000 Census (one week) and the manager of a Subway restaurant (one week). All this followed a six month stint as a line worker at a filing cabinet factory in Big Rapids, Michigan, where I had spent my days taking file drawers off hooks and sending them down conveyor belts to some mysterious location. Surely this, too, would come and go quickly.

But I liked the work and I liked the people, so I stayed—for well over three years. In a work force of 35 cabinet makers, sanders, cutters, sweepers, and repair personnel, I was one of three native English speakers. My co-workers were from Mexico, Guatemala, Sicily, Albania, and Palestine. Initially I worked alongside a man from the little mountain town of Topia in Durango, Mexico. My classroom Spanish allowed us to interact and learn a bit about each other as we rubbed spots of overspray from each cabinet surface—the repetition allowed plenty of time for conversation.

Getting to know him was a delight, and he taught me a reflective poem that he wrote that I return to frequently nearly 20 years later. Over the course of the next several months, I continued to form similar relationships during the work and the breaks.

As I grew in my cabinet making skills and moved on from cleaning glue to building cabinets, the cast of characters I was able to work with and interact with also grew. Within a few months of beginning at the cabinet shop and learning the stories of some of my coworkers, it became clear among our very diverse group of acquaintances that we were having a powerful experience of cultural encounter. We were privileged to learn about cultures that could potentially have been sealed off from us had it not been for our common work, a prevailing kindness among us, and our mutual eagerness to improve our language skills—and, frequently, our ability simply to listen to each other.

At a certain point in our developing friendships, my coworkers and I began to exchange musical selections on cassette tapes. A particularly good friend of mine gave me a copy of *Uniendo Fronteras* ("uniting borders") by Los Tigres del Norte, a popular Norteño band from Mexico. I listened with delight—until I heard the following lyrics:

| | |
|---|---|
| *Y si no miente la historia* | *And if history doesn't lie* |
| *Aquí se sentó en la gloria* | *Here sat in its glory* |
| *La poderosa nación* | *A powerful nation* |
| *Entre guerreros valientes* | *Among valiant warriors* |
| *Indios de dos continentes* | *Indians from two continents* |
| *Mezclados con español* | *Mixed with Spanish* |
| *Y si a los siglos nos vamos* | *And if we go to the centuries* |
| *Somos más americanos* | *We are more American* |
| *Somos más americanos* | *We are more American* |
| *Que el hijo de anglo-sajón.* | *Than the son of the Anglo-Saxon.** |

* Los Tigres del Norte, "Somos Más Americanos," from *Uniendo Fronteras* (Fonovisa, 2001). My paraphrase.

As a "son of the Anglo-Saxon" if ever there was one, I was startled out of my naiveté quickly: while we were becoming friends on one level, there existed beneath our friendship the weight of a violent and difficult history. The clash of European and Mesoamerican cultures over the past 500 or so years moved beneath our interactions like the sea beneath a boat—generally calm, but potentially stormy. We could work well together, go to parties together, chat comfortably—but our present-day encounter was complicated by the *history* of our cultural contexts.

When I asked my friend about the song "Somos Mas Americanos," he said, "es una canción, no mas"—"it's just a song." I suspected then, however, and continue to believe, that the song's lyrics represented something compelling: the power of history stretching into the present. Our encounter was submerged within the Encounter, and to take our difficult history seriously meant that I had to admit that *at one level* I represented and resembled the agents who had caused his ancestors incredible pain—and who continued to discriminate and marginalize people like him into the present day. History had an influence on us that we did not choose—and could not choose to ignore. From a historical perspective, our friendship was in some ways exceptional—and this fact made it all the more valuable (I believe) to each of us.

In retrospect and with the aid of additional reflection on these encounters, I have been able to identify stages of development in my personal cultural encounter. In the early stages, a tendency to romanticize the culturally other prevailed. Growth into deeper relationships across cultural differences replaced this romantic veil with a more authentic appreciation.

In spite of learning how to categorize my experience of cultural encounter, however, I have never been able completely to discover the source of its awesome power. The sensation of standing at the brink of a vast sea of difference—not "mere" differences in language or looks or location—has stayed with me ever since I worked at the cabinet shop. Each time I speak with someone from a different cultural background from my own, I sense this same awe waking up in me, drawing me to an awareness of profound power. Cultural encounter—an encounter with a human being which fully engages the sincere and irreducible differences among people from different backgrounds—is humbling and instructive. It challenges our attempts to describe it. It sometimes demands silence.

The intercultural friendships which grew over the years at the cabinet shop represent the genesis of this book. My experience at the shop set me on an eclectic and perhaps idiosyncratic search for literary and theological works that signaled a similar appreciation for the role of such encounters in understanding the Self and the Other. The work of Sor Juana Inés de la Cruz has proved to be just such a source. As I have engaged with Sor Juana's writing and her life, I have become increasingly convinced that her seventeenth-century insights into the dynamics of culture, knowledge, and vocation have a great deal to do with present-day cultural encounters. I sincerely hope that others will find her to be as heartening a companion in their own journeys as I have found her to be in my own.

# Acknowledgements

This book began as a doctoral dissertation at the Lutheran School of Theology at Chicago, and I am grateful for the support of my teachers, colleagues, and friends at that school. I am particularly thankful for the encouragement of my mentor and advisor, Peter Vethanayagamony.

Before this was a dissertation project, however, this work began as a reflection on real-world relationships that I have been privileged to form over the years. I am grateful for many memorable conversations with my coworkers on the grounds crew of Princeton Theological Seminary in New Jersey and at Ros's Cabinets in Romeo, Michigan, especially Javier Torres, Manuel Ayala, and Ricardo Alonso Garduño.

More recently, my work at the Episcopal Church of the Redeemer/Iglesia Episcopal El Redentor in Elgin, Illinois, has given me the opportunity to form and develop cross-cultural relationships. It is a joy and a true privilege to accompany this congregation in their life together.

I appreciate the helpful feedback provided by Robert Warski, who read significant parts of the manuscript.

I am very grateful to the editors at Political Animal Press and thank them for making this book possible. Alex Wall and Lewis Slawsky have helped me clarify and focus the ideas explored in the dissertation and have taught me a great deal about the processes of writing, rewriting, and publication.

Adam Mawer has been extremely helpful as I have learned how to present the ideas of the book in various forms and formats.

My family has provided tremendous support and encouragement throughout writing of this book, too, and I am immensely thankful for their curiosity, interest, and care.

My sons Oscar and Rowan have been living with this project ever since it began as a "gissertation." I am profoundly thankful for their love, patience, and interest in my work, and I hope that their own friendships throughout life are deepened by the gift of cultural encounter.

Finally, to my wife, Lily, te agradezco con todo mi corazón el apoyo, amor, y motivación que me has brindado.

# Introduction

Interest in Sor Juana has surged in recent years—and it is easy to see why. Sor Juana was a brilliant and unapologetic polymath, and her keen gaze roamed over dozens of diverse and fascinating subjects. That makes it easy for readers with a diversity of interests to find something in Sor Juana that speaks directly to their questions. Sor Juana wrote about religion, colonial politics, epistemology, culture—but also Egyptology, science, cooking, music theory, and more. She had a sharp wit, a clever and incisive way with words, and a confident self-awareness that lends her voice a compelling authenticity. She is a delight to read, and to the extent that we can know someone so vastly separated from us in time and space, a delight to meet.

Because Sor Juana can be legitimately approached from such a wide variety of disciplinary angles, and because curiosity about her so richly rewards readers from many backgrounds, it is crucial to construct any study of Sor Juana by first narrowing and naming the particular concerns of the approach. This book develops a constellation of claims based on Sor Juana's life and work, focusing especially on three primary aspects: her location between cultures, her ability to navigate diverse ways of knowing between these cultures, and her ability to intervene in ongoing conversations about the role of gender and identity as they pertain to public discourse. This book seeks to demonstrate how Sor Juana's life and work both embody and clearly articulate the tensions and opportunities that arise from the phenomenon of cultural encounter, which I define as the moment (prolonged or otherwise) when individuals or groups of people from radically different backgrounds—cultures—come face to face with each other. This "facing" can be precipitated by myriad factors, and in some ways the means which move people into such encounters is of less interest here than the way the encounters themselves then unfold.

Sor Juana lived at a time when colonization and global exploration among European powers was precipitating cultural encounters throughout the world. These encounters were marked on the one hand by giddy enthusiasm on the part of many who believed that "new" worlds were being discovered—and were met with wonder (at best) and abject terror (at worst) by those who were "found" and often eventually colonized. By the time Sor Juana was writing, the encounter between Europe and present-day Mexico had been underway for a century, but was no less confusing, cacophonous, violent, and occasionally even thrilling than it had been when Cortes first set foot in Mesoamerica in 1519. She found a way to live and write between these cultures and within this profound mixing of human concerns and struggles. The fact that the reverberations of the European colonial impulse still affect public consciousness, global economics, and individual subjectivity up to the present indicate the importance of Sor Juana's insights into the present day.

## Who was Sor Juana?

Sor Juana Inés de la Cruz was born in the small town of San Miguel de Nepantla, Amecameca, in what is now central Mexico and was at the time the Spanish colony known simply as Nueva España—New Spain. There is some question as to the exact date of her birth, either 1648 or 1651, birthdate conventions having been more fluid then than they are today, and various factors influenced the dating process. As the child of unmarried parents, there was probably later some equivocation about the precise details of her birth in order to seek admission into strict religious orders.[1] But baptism records seem to suggest the earlier date, and most recent scholarship accepts 1648 as most likely.

Her given name was Juana Inés de Asbaje y Ramírez de Santillana. Her father, Pedro Manuel de Asbaje y Vargas Machuca, was a military officer from the Basque region of Spain. Juana's mother, Isabel Ramírez de Santillana, was a criolla (a Spaniard born within the colony).[2] On both her parents' sides, then, Sor Juana was directly connected to Spain, a connection which shaped her writerly voice and generally European sense of readership throughout her career. Though born in the colonial world of New Spain, her roots were across the ocean in Europe.

Most of her upbringing took place in the neighboring town of Panoayan, where her maternal grandparents took care of her. Juana was a precocious and driven child. She had learned to read by the time she was three,[3] displaying from an early age her exceptional language skills and a voracious appetite for learning and reading. She lived in the world of words right from the start. This fascination with language eventually provided her with the key notion informing her sense of vocation—the desire for knowledge, which in her native Spanish comes across even more succinctly and passionately—her *desear saber.*

By the time she was 13, Juana's extraordinary intellectual gifts were readily apparent and began to be the subject of public praise. She went to live in the residential complex maintained by the viceroy, Don Antonio Sebastián de Toledo Molina y Salazar, and his wife, Doña Leonor Carreto. The viceroy in the colony governed in place of the king and represented royal authority through his person and surrounding court. For children closely connected to Spanish families, especially children who showed unusual intellectual promise, providing an education was an expected contribution to the national and colonial cause. A colony was more than economy—it was also a place to showcase the culture of the colonizing force. Education helped further this process. Juana became one of the children formed by the viceroy's education program. It changed her life completely: given the large and well-connected audience of the viceregal residence and court, Juana was thrust into the world of manners, letters, intrigue, and the subtlety of interpersonal rivalries. She was a perfect fit.

Juana's cleverness and linguistic ability earned attention and favor during the several years she spent in the viceregal court of the Spanish government in Mexico City.[4] And although situated in the colony, the court's attention was aimed toward Spain. The ambitious understood and worked with this Iberian orientation. More than simply the seat of government, the viceregal residence in the colony of Nueva España was Spain's effort to make the "new" world in some way resemble the developing national identity of its old-world colonizers.

In the rapidly changing world of the developing colony, images of a gold-encrusted Spanish court leant a sense of importance and place to a context that was otherwise chaotic, conflicted, and probably very tense. In an environment such as this, with its reality rooted in the colony and its imagery linked to the best possible version of Spain's glory, young Juana learned to divide her attention. She learned how to live in the colony while simultaneously attending to the fashions and cultural expectations of courtly Spain. This dual reality and the literary vision that it engendered could have been awkward, but in time Juana was able to embrace and appreciate this position between. Her work is wedged between the world of Iberian cultural preferences and the striking images of the Aztec culture prevalent in central Mexico.[5] The massive cultural encounter around her provided her with a dynamic mix of images. And Juana was the ideal candidate to explore and navigate the tensions inherent in this meeting of disparate worlds.

As Juana grew up in and was formed by the viceregal court

grew, she naturally faced decisions about what to do with her life. Two options presented themselves to her (and to other women of her family/social status): marriage or convent life. Both, interestingly, required a dowry and social standing, so there was little financial reason to prefer one over the other. Already firmly committed to a life of writing and learning, Juana could see that marriage was likely to impinge on her goals. So she (as with many others) explored ways to channel her gifts into the societally accepted trajectory of convent life.

Not all convents were equally congenial to her, however. Convents existed on a continuum from more to less rigorous. Some were quite strict, others were more permissive. Juana first tried a convent with a rigidly interpreted community rule, but eventually opted for the more open schedule of a less intensely structured convent. She wanted time to study and write, after all, and not every convent could offer such an opportunity. When she eventually took her religious vows, it was in "the Order of St. Jerome in the convent of St. Paula, where she became a professed nun on February 24, 1669."[6] She took the name Sor ("sister") Juana Inés de la Cruz: Juana of the Cross.

Sor Juana's choice for the convent of St. Paula had everything to do with her desire to commit to full-time—seemingly perpetual—reading and writing.[7] Her work as a writer was becoming increasingly important to her. But her charisma and intelligence led to other opportunities, as well. She grew in responsibility within her convent, becoming the account keeper for the group. She leveraged her resources to assemble a considerable library in her quarters—no small feat in colonial New Spain, where books were rare and expensive. She even had a servant girl, so her cloistered life was far from austere. She had ample time and resources. Visiting conversation partners (both from church and the viceregal court) kept her connected with the world outside of the convent, which she virtually never left. All of the pieces were in place to allow her to engage her intellectual gifts in earnest.

And she did. Sor Juana wrote and wrote, frequently at the invitation of others. Many of her early publications were commissions for religious ceremonial events. In many public liturgies of the time, blank spaces within a particular church service would be filled with devotions or religious poetry, even drama. These intertemporal pieces became an expected and structured part of religious services. It was common for pieces to be commissioned to fill these spots, and Sor Juana showed great talent for writing them. Her early work was done at the request of the Church, in conversation with the Church, and in harmony with the goals of the Church.

Sor Juana's liturgical poetry became famous—literally famous—on both sides of the Atlantic.

Sor Juana's poetic and dramatic work was enthusiastically commissioned for public events, religious ceremonies, and devotional sequences. As she grew as a writer, Sor Juana became involved in new and more challenging conversations. This wasn't always by choice, as others sometimes thrust her into the spotlight without warning. The conversations that she eventually entered went beyond the decorative function of much of her early writing. She entered into substantive conversations about sermons, theology, orthodoxy, and the dynamics of the colony itself. Sor Juana studied theological material on her own, but the public shift in her writing from poetic and dramatic works to overtly theological argumentation was the result of the machinations of others.

The 1690 unintended publication of a critique of a sermon by a famous preacher signaled her entry into a new kind of conversation. A bishop who admired Sor Juana and occasionally visited her requested that she record some of her observations regarding the text of a sermon preached by Portuguese Jesuit Antonio Vieira (1608-1697). This bishop, the Bishop of Puebla, Don Miguel Fernández de Santa Cruz y Sahagún, took these observations and published them under the title: Carta Atenagórica, or "letter worthy of Athena." Flattering title aside, the work was apparently published without Sor Juana's express permission. And in addition, the bishop appended his own letter to Sor Juana's observations. But he did not sign it as "Bishop of Puebla." Rather, he signed his appended letter as "Sor Filotea de la Cruz"—the fictitious name of a concerned fellow nun. This Sor Filotea (really the bishop) was greatly concerned that Sor Juana's writing was becoming too secular, too daring. Sor Juana had left the proper subject of her work—her own salvation—and had begun to meddle. The Bishop of Puebla—for whatever reason, and there are probably several—donned the mask of a fellow sister and admonished Sor Juana to theological and ecclesiastical conversations well enough alone.

The eventual fallout of the bishop's censorial game may have contributed to Sor Juana's complete literary silence after 1692.[8] Before her silence, though, the bishop's provocative move occasioned her most famous work—her "Respuesta" or "Answer" to Sor Filotea. It is probably impossible to recover the precise chain of events that surrounded Sor Juana's final silence. Many factors converged. In any case, the writerly gifts that had up until then gained her fame and notoriety ceased amid Church controversy. She famously signed—in her own blood—a renunciation of her work as a theologian, naming herself "la peor de todas"—"the worst of all." Apparently cowed, Sor Juana died on April 17, 1695, at the age of forty-six, while caring for other nuns taken ill by an epidemic.

## Theological and Cultural Themes in Sor Juana's Works

Sor Juana's 1690 sermon critique and subsequent defense is the most overtly theological of her writings. Nevertheless, her poetry and drama can as easily be mined for theological themes. Her image-rich poetry and innovative use of established dramatic forms present theological and other material in a less propositional but equally forthright manner as her theological prose. Her acute theological sense is combined with an awareness of her writerly location between the literary preferences of Spain and the cultural images of Mesoamerica. Others—both in Spain and in New Spain—saw her in this interstitial space, as well: in the emblematic frontispiece to a collection of her work titled *Fama, y obras póstumas del fénix de Mexico, decima musa, poetisa americana Sor Juana Inés de la Cruz*, a picture of Sor Juana occupies a position between personifications of Mesoamerican ethnicity and culture on the one hand and Iberian/European ethnicity and culture on the other. She holds a plumed pen in her hand, apparently ready to compose from her position between these two representations. A host of other emblematic details crowd the frontispiece, each adding an interpretive note to the general image of a writer working within the encounter between two vastly different cultures.

It is unknowable to what extent Sor Juana considered her projects to be the unification, preservation, or mutual appreciation of these distinct cultures. Some scholarship interprets portions of her work as intended (as with Bartolomé de las Casas a century before) to preserve Aztec and Mesoamerican culture from devaluation and underestimation on the part of the Spanish. In other words, her work may have been aimed at an Iberian audience (whether in Madrid or in the vice-regal courts of Mexico City) with cultural apology as a significant goal.[9] Or it may have been aimed primarily at those who would limit her and other women's ability to participate in theological discourse. She certainly did some of her very best work when arguing for women's rights to education and participation in theological discourse. Her works in both areas—cultural defense and gender advocacy—show Sor Juana to be an *occasional* writer—that is, her writing responded to occasions, challenges, and opportunities rather than circling around or carefully developing particular themes or concentrations over the course of a career.

We are left with the image of a writer whose gifts gained her fame and controversy. All of what she wrote is located at the meeting of the cultural tectonic plates of her time: the culture of Spain interacting with Aztec culture, the reality of colonial brutality interacting with the missional zeal of the church, and the reality of vocational gifts in tension with established gender roles in church and society. In much of her work, Sor Juana worked within established genres and roles. But she also expanded these categories. She pushed poetic and dramatic genres past previously seen limits. And she challenged the Church to grapple with its prohibitions against women's participation in theological discourse. As is often the case, Sor Juana's challenges to power structures led to controversy. What she saw and said reaches into the realm of universal (or at least continuing) conversations around truth, how truth is known, and how human individuals and cultures navigate one of life's most exciting and puzzling features: our differences.

## Note on the Definition of Culture used in this Book

A central trope used throughout this book is the notion of "cultural encounter." Cultural encounter is not merely an abstraction. As a general concept, it depends on two imprecise but meaningful definitions: a definition of "culture" and a definition of "encounter." Among the many definitions of culture on offer, that developed by theologian and cultural analyst Robert J. Schreiter in his seminal book *Constructing Local Theologies* is thorough and has been proved useful by many scholars. Depending heavily on the work of American anthropologist Clifford Geertz, Schreiter develops a complex definition of culture that includes the complete systems of images, linguistic patterns, practices, behaviors, preferences, and life-strategies that form and permeate human life.[10] Cultures tend to develop within and partly in interaction with geographic areas. In addition to geographic and political borders, cultural boundaries are often signaled by differences in language.

Cultural encounter takes place when persons formed in distinct and discrete cultural milieus are brought into some form of relationship with one another. This happens either by choice or by force. In cultural encounters, persons are faced with the necessity of navigating their relationship through pinch-points of cultural discontinuity or even incompatibility. Past events such as (im)migration, colonization, religious campaigns, pilgrimage, trade, and war are equally at play in creating the conditions for cultural encounter as are their present-day corollaries. In daily life, many people encounter many *peoples*—sometimes these encounters can be assigned to past events, sometimes to present events. In each case, though, the history of cultural formation is operative. When cultural differences attend these meetings, unfamiliar lines of code are set into motion, self-awareness and self-consciousness may rise, and a sense of dislocation may creep in.

It is impossible and sometimes even irresponsible to speak of a particular culture in a generalized or generalizing way. No culture can be named simply or unproblematically. There are always exceptions and subcultures within any given group. And as anyone knows who watches new words appear each year in dictionaries, culture is constantly changing. It resists definitive characterization. Nevertheless, this is the shorthand that we have at our disposal, and so with these cautions in mind, throughout this book I will refer to European, Spanish, Iberian, Mesoamerican, Aztec/Nahua *cultures*—fully aware that this usage is complicated.

# Chapter 1

## Sor Juana Between Worlds: Spain and New Spain

| | |
|---|---|
| *¿Pues no ves la impropiedad* | *But does it not seem ill-advised* |
| *De que en Méjico se escriba* | *That what you write in Mexico* |
| *Y en Madrid se represente?* | *Be represented in Madrid?* |

—*Loa Para el Auto sacramental* El divino Narciso[11]

### Sor Juana in Historical Context: Facing Spain

One of the central truths of Sor Juana's life and work can be captured in a single claim: she lived *between worlds.* She grew up in an American colony of a European nation. Her language, religion, and literary points of reference were all fundamentally transplanted from Spain. Spain gave her her name, the basic principles underlying her education, and her social circle. Her geographical home, though, was Mesoamerican, and the tension between her cultural and physical location affected her deeply. As she was becoming a writer, Sor Juana's audience was split between the colony of New Spain and Spain itself. In each case, her work and her readership were essentially European while influenced by their Mesoamerican colonial surroundings.

### *Historical and Political Realities in Spain*

Spain was going through tremendous changes before and during Sor Juana's lifetime. The seventeenth century found Spain struggling with its developing identity as a recently-unified nation. Smaller kingdoms within the nation continued to generate their own claims to allegiance, loyalty, and identity formation. What's more, Spain was constantly struggling with its relationship to its far-flung colony (proudly called "New Spain") in the Americas. The so-called discovery of the American continent went through dramatic transitions: what had started as an economic and spiritual windfall had by Sor Juana's time become an economic, ethical, and logistical albatross. Sor Juana in New Spain was living in the conflicted colonial space that Spain continued to try to understand and control.

The initial encounter with the "new" world—roughly the latter part of the fifteenth century and into the sixteenth century—found Spain in desperate financial and political straits. It was also entering a phase in which its sense of national unity and identity would for programmatic and political reasons become a significant concern.[12] This was due in part to the many wars and battles Spain was engaged in throughout Europe.[13] Primary among these, and just prior to the first encounter with the "new" world, was a series of civil wars within Spain itself related to succession (1464-1480). During the decades which followed the initial encounter with the Americas, Spain continued to struggle with this issue and how to exert control over its territories throughout Europe, as well as with its near neighbors, France and Portugal. Significant (and expensive) conflicts included Spain's attempt to control the Western Mediterranean through Naples (1495), skirmishes with the French and within the Netherlands throughout the middle of the sixteenth century, and, most importantly, the Thirty Years' War (1618-1648). During Sor Juana's lifetime, Portugal had its independence recognized (1668), and the pieces were in place by the end of her life (1695) for yet another series of wars of succession (1700-1714).

Spain also underwent a massive shift in political and religious leadership. After hundreds of years of Muslim rule, Christian monarchs "re-conquered" the Iberian Peninsula in a process culminating at Granada in 1492. The combination of economic stress, the development of the Iberian Peninsula as a nominally Christian zone, and a variety of powerful movements within the artistic and literary worlds each influenced how Sor Juana developed her voice and cultivated her readership.

### *Holy Struggle as Backdrop to Sor Juana's Work: The Reconquista (722-1492)*

Names of historical periods often reveal particular perspectives, allegiances, and assumptions. Such is the case with the phenomenon in Spain called the *Reconquista*. This way of periodizing history assumes that Christian presence in Spain is normative and that the 700 years of Muslim rule were exceptional and unwelcome. In other words, it is not a neutral term. In any case, though, it is commonly used, and refers to events that had much to do with how Sor Juana lived and worked.

The "re-" conquest of Spain started almost immediately after the initial entry of Muslims into the Iberian Peninsula. It might be imagined as a reflexive "pushing back" against the new inhabitants. With the Muslim invasion (again, not a neutral term) in 711, the Visigothic lands of what is now Spain began a transition from a generally Christian province to an area ruled and populated by followers of Islam.[14] Keeping in mind that at this point the Prophet Mohammed's teachings had only been promulgated for about 100 years, this missionary success and military/political takeover is nothing short of astonishing. Prior to the arrival of Islam, Visigothic kings and chieftains of the Iberian Peninsula had been weakened by their own internal feuding. Nurturing these internal disputes allowed the Muslim invaders to divide and conquer.[15] Competing claimants to authority diffused power: "the invasion of 711 coincided with the civil war that resulted from the election of Roderic."[16] This civil war was a vulnerability the Muslims easily exploited, and their invasion of Spain was swift.

As early as 718, however, and by all accounts by 722, various Christian groups in the northern reaches of the Iberian Peninsula had begun to encroach on Muslim territory. Thus began the so-called *Reconquista*—clearly as named from the Christian point of view, as noted above. The *Reconquista* lasted for centuries. It passed through phases of greater or lesser intensity and evolved over time. Therefore it is not reducible to a simple characterization. Nevertheless it is helpful to see its basic contours: "...the idea of the *Reconquista* [was] a *sustained holy struggle* aimed at recovering a land which had been lost by its *legitimate* rulers after the Muslim conquest."[17]

This "holy struggle" and the idea of "legitimate rule" fostered the development of a mythical unified past in Spain. The process of imagining a reconquest, after all, depends on a sense that there is something held *in common* that needs to be recovered. This idea had consequences during the expansion of Spain as a colonizing force in the sixteenth century. Fractured groups retold their story as one of unity in the face of incursion. The *Reconquista* would continue with various degrees of effectiveness and haste for the next several centuries, gradually making its way through the kingdoms in the north toward the south in 1492.

Like any cultural narrative, the story of the *Reconquista* became populated with certain character types. Some of those who emerged during this struggle become durable enough to influence the eventual "conquest" and early colonizing efforts of the Americas. Among these is the cult of the heroic Christian warrior.[18] Because Spain during these centuries was not a united kingdom (but rather a loose conglomeration of smaller kingdoms), local leaders and rulers exerted a great deal of power within their spheres of influence and control. Without a strong national identity and without a strong localized government, local kings within the Spanish territories could parlay the capture of small territories into the construction of large legends of their heroism and military might. Kings commanding even small armies in the northern parts of Spain—particularly in Navarre and the Basque region, and stretching west toward Compostella—became the subjects of Christian cults of personality. Their faith—a crucial component in a holy war—was revered alongside their military might.

Religious orders were founded in the wake of the *Reconquista*, further elevating the myth of the warrior-class clergy and saints.[19] Invocation of St. Isidore of Seville (among the great personalities of the Visigothic kingdom prior to the Muslim incursion) and a supposed Visigothic unity[20] within the Iberian Peninsula were added to this volatile mix, furthering the notion that true heroism was an amalgamation of devout faith and military prowess.[21] In reality, the most by way of unity that Isidore of Seville (c. 560 – 636) accomplished was the unification of the Iberian kingdoms under the Roman legal system—but in terms of actual power and identity, each small kingdom from Granada to Navarre was essentially its own political entity.[22] Nevertheless, the image of Isidore and the idea of unity were powerfully motivating, and the *Reconquista* and all of its various trajectories were fueled by the image of the warrior saint reestablishing *limpieza de sangre* ("purity of blood") on the Iberian Peninsula.

The northern parts of Spain (which were under Muslim influence for the shortest period of time) became a source for both the military power and the myth-building power of the *Reconquista,* as well as its eventual ability to push the Muslim rulers from Granada in 1492. The development of the cult of St. James (Santiago) and the establishment of the pilgrimage site at Santiago de Compostella in northwest Spain further strengthened the myth-making on the part of the Christian forces in Spain. This version of Santiago (a conflation of both James the Greater and James the Less, according to Mexican observer Carlos Fuentes) was reputed to have been a military expert whose mere presence caused Muslims to flee.[23] The iconography around Santiago (as featured in later depictions) shows him mounted on a powerful war horse and armed in the full metal armor of a well-funded knight. Pilgrimages to Santiago de Compostella became common and fueled the quest for a "return" to a unified Christian Spain.[24] The fact that such an entity existed only in legend notwithstanding, this rhetoric found wide acceptance and was used in the propaganda supporting the *Reconquista.*

By the late 1400's, the Muslim kingdoms of the Iberian Peninsula had fallen one by one to their Christian re-conquerors.[25] The Muslim kings and leaders had in turn succumbed to infighting and quarreling amongst themselves, and thus the Christian armies were more easily able to divide them and drive them further south. This division on the part of the Muslims—reminiscent of the division among the Visigothic kings who had fallen to them in 711—led to a peculiar feature of the last stages of the *Reconquista* with implications for a discussion of the colonizing process in the Americas: the Muslims who were displaced from their seats of power often took to the mountains and hills of southern Spain, especially in the region of Extremadura and in the northern sections of Granada. The guerrilla warfare that followed upended the traditional "etiquette" of warfare used by the Christian armies. No longer did army face army on a well-defined field, and no longer did the siege of city walls define the last stages of a particular battle.[26] Instead, small groups of warriors would meet and skirmish in ill-defined spaces, forcing the Christian warriors to adjust their techniques.[27] This object lesson in guerrilla warfare affected the later conquest of the Americas, since with few exceptions, the battles with the Indigenous peoples promulgated by Hernan

Cortés (1485-1547) and his ilk took place away from cities and well-defined fields of battle.

### *The Reconquista and the "New" World*

The last stages of the *Reconquista* provided mythology (the warrior saint), training (the skirmishes of the final press toward Granada from 1482 to 1492), and the identity for persons wishing to serve God and country. It also codified and centralized the idea of *purity*. This notion was expressed through the idea of *limpieza de sangre*—purity or "cleanliness" of blood. This constellation of characteristics would morph into the *Conquistador* in the conquest of the Americas, a character type destined to populate narratives of the colonization of New Spain.

The myth of Spanish unity took concrete steps toward becoming reality with the marriage of Isabella (of the kingdom of Castile) and Ferdinand (of the kingdom of Aragon) in 1469.[28] Eventually each of these rulers inherited their particular "mini" kingdom. Their combined holdings gave Spain its closest approximation to national unity in its history. This move toward unification fed the narrative of nationalism and energized the final stages of the *Reconquista*. In January of 1492, the final press of the Christian armies defeated the Muslim forces at Granada and saw them retreat across the Straits of Gibraltar into northern Africa. Within this same year, Ferdinand and Isabel also privately financed the voyage of Cristobal Colón—Christopher Columbus—to find a new route to the Indies. Before news of his adventures had returned to the Spanish monarchs, the king and queen attempted to realize the idea of *limpieza de sangre* by expelling the Jews from Spain.

This ill-advised move led to significant urban depopulation and a severe financial crisis. This in turn led to the awkward combination of a triumphalist religious motif in the Church, a proud nationalism developing in society, and a massive financial shortfall in the state.[29] When Cristobal Colón reported the "discovery" of new and wealthy realms in the West, Ferdinand and Isabella believed that their financial troubles had been miraculously solved.[30] Colón sent his initial reports to Barcelona, where Ferdinand and Isabella were at the time. His first reports focused especially on the apparent health of the Indigenous persons, the apparent wealth present, and the need to claim both persons (as subjects) and the wealth for Spain. The monarchs, keenly aware of Portugal's explorers following closely behind Colón, wrote to Pope Alexander VI—who happened to be a Spaniard—whose bull *Inter caetera* in 1493 assured Spain (as well as Portugal, leading to the eventual formation of Brazil) of its claim to the Americas. In order to exploit this newfound wealth, however, the monarchs needed to employ persons with a peculiar mix of skills and qualifications.

First, the candidates needed to be "old Christian," possessing *limpieza de sangre*. Second, they needed to be courageous, familiar with physical privation and danger, and motivated by a noble zeal for the causes of Church and state. Finally, the candidates for this work needed to be willing to take on massive financial risks of their own. The monarchs were unable to provide actual payment and funding up front, so those sent to the "new" world would need to be paid on the promise of recompense from the spoils of their journeys. Other readers of this moment have seen clearly the continuity between the *Reconquista* and the colonization of the Americas:

> [T]he *Reconquista* provided a useful precedent. It had been the practice for the Crown to make contracts with leaders of military expeditions against the Moors. It seems probable that these contracts inspired the document known as the *capitulación,* which later became the customary form of agreement between the Spanish Crown and the *Conquistadores* of America.[31]

The hardy and faithful "warrior saint" constructed by the *Recon-*

*quista* fit Spain's economic and iconic needs perfectly and leads into the image of the *Conquistadores.*

Although several less-famous *Conquistadores* followed the initial rush to the Americas after Columbus, the relationship between Mexico and Spain was most fundamentally affected by the person (and the legend) of Hernán Cortés. From a base on the island of Cuba, Cortés learned of an even greater land mass to the south and west. Along with a group of men selected for the journey, Cortés reconnoitered the eastern shores of present-day Mexico and eventually learned of the population center in Mexico City/Tenochtitlan. Returning later in 1519, Cortés met Montezuma and his Aztec ambassadors on Maundy Thursday.[32]

Peaceful at first, this relationship quickly turned sour. The *noche triste* or "sorrowful night" saw the visitors from Spain expelled from Mexico City/Tenochtitlan, and Cortés and his men soon returned to give battle.[33] The theme of division among the conquered emerges here, too, just as it did with the Visigothic kings and the Muslim kings in Granada. The Aztec Empire had been consolidated hastily through powerful takeovers of smaller and less bellicose tribes. The city of Tenochtitlan, built in the midst of Lake Taxcoco in what is now Mexico City, was the seat of an Aztec Empire with many enemies and discontented subjects. Cortés manipulated these disputes and deputized many smaller bands of Indigenous people against the Aztecs, and by 1521 his victory was complete.

Powerful symbols with resonance into our own times emerged from this conquest. First, it is worth noting that the initial representatives of European presence in Mesoamerica were those formed in the mold of warrior saints, the *Conquistadores*: the first representatives were perhaps inclined to interpret difference as a threat and to view violence as a normal response to that threat. Second, the initial encounter between European and Mesoamerican people groups involved long-lasting and eventually mythified conflicts around gender roles. This is evident in the case of La

Malinche, the Indigenous girl "given" to Cortés as his companion and as translator. It is clear that the girl known as La Malinche could not have withstood the pressures of those who "gave" her or those (Cortés and his men) who "took" her. And yet in the emerging mythology of Mexico, she (the one who was betrayed by her people) was seen as the *betrayer* of the Indigenous people. She came to symbolize the failure of the Indigenous people to claim their own agency during the conquest of their land. Although there may not be direct continuity between Sor Juana and La Malinche, the very fact of this complicated and gendered history in New Spain will have implications for Sor Juana as she works to defend her vocation as a theologian and writer.

## *Nuestra Señora de Guadalupe* as Cross-Cultural Religious Symbol

Religious tension was at the heart of the encounter between Spanish and Indigenous people groups. The spiritual conquest of the Mexican portion of Mesoamerica gave rise to powerful symbols of religious syncretism.[34] The Aztec gods Huitzilopochtli and Quetzalcoatl—themselves appropriated by the conquering Aztecs—became conflated with various legends of the Christian saints. The best-known instance of this syncretism is the Virgin of Guadalupe, in which the Aztec goddess Tonantzin became linked to a particular apparition of the Virgin Mary in 1531.[35] Beginning on December 9, 1531, a mere 10 years after the fall of Tenochtitlán, Juan Diego's (1474-1548) experience of Tonantzin/Mary on her hill at Tepayec incorporated *flor y canto* (an aesthetic way of knowing divine truth), healing, Indigenous iconography, racial inclusiveness, and the ultimate "conversion" of Church authorities to an Indigenous way of experiencing the divine. Juan Diego's story begins with hearing music as he passes Tepayec, and when he investigates the source of the music, he sees Tonantzin/Mary.

She asks him to tell the Bishop of the diocese of her presence, and on two occasions Juan Diego does precisely that.

On his third trip past the hill at Tepayec, on his way to secure medical help for his dying uncle, Juan Diego again encounters Tonantzin/Mary. He confesses his haste and anxiety, to which she asks him in Nahuatl, "Am I not here who am your Mother?" Juan Diego confesses, too, that he has been unable to convince the Bishop of her presence—so she gives him a sign. She asks him to pick a large number of roses growing on the hill—appearing out of season—and to take them in his *tilma* or cloak to show the Bishop. When he follows her instructions and arrives at the Bishop's seat, his unfolding *tilma* reveals a beautiful image of la Virgin imprinted on its fibers. La Virgin is clothed in a *reboso* (the typical dress of the Indigenous people), has dark skin, and has revealed herself in the native language of Nahuatl. Given these signs, the Bishop himself comes to believe Juan Diego's story and orders the construction of a church at Tepayec. When Juan Diego opened his *tilma* for the Bishop in December of that year, it signaled the beginning of the "pushing back" of the Indigenous culture against its European conquerors. This event continues to be a central reference point for historical and religious reflection (not to mention a lively devotional focus) up to the present day.[36]

Meanwhile, in Spain, the formation of a national identity continued apace.[37] The "discovery" of a new world fed the well-established notion of *limpieza de sangre* as well as the emerging (and more generally European) notion of a utopia.[38] In Spain, the notion of utopia (ironically, "no place") fired the popular imagination with stories of the "new world." It was easy to leap to an idealization of this "no place" as a new Eden. Thus religious and sociological elements joined with the economic pressures which drove the monarchs to fund the *Conquistadores* through the promise of land grants and subjects to work them. This system was known as the *encomienda*.[39]

The *encomienda* was fraught with religious and imperialistic assumptions. Queen Isabella in 1503 instituted the *encomienda* system in a letter. In this letter she lamented that the "great freedom" that the "Indians" enjoyed was preventing them from becoming Christians, a process which she envisioned as resulting from daily life and interaction with other (Spanish) Christians. Thus she imagined the *encomiendas* as an *enclosed and salubrious* social system in which the Indians could "work the island [of Hispaniola], populate it, make it fruitful, and gather the gold that is there so that these my neighbors might benefit from it." Evidently the similarities between this supposedly helpful arrangement and outright slavery were not apparent to the queen. The letter authorized the colonists "to compel and force these Indians to deal and converse with the Christians on that island and work in its buildings and gather gold and other metals and do farm work and maintenance for the Christians who live on that island; and to arrange that each one be paid a daily wage and maintenance according to the quality of the land and the person and the work..." She further added that the Indians were not to be mistreated, though this tenet was difficult to enforce and was frequently (and tragically) ignored.

The economic pressures that led Spain to its fevered colonization of New Spain/Mexico eventually led to Spain's dependency on the colony and a reversal of the initial high hopes for an external economic boost. By the time Sor Juana was born in 1648, Spain itself was miserably dependent on silver income from across the Atlantic. This dependency deeply affected the world in which Sor Juana came to understand and portray the encounter between the Iberian and the Mesoamerican cultures. Spain's dependence on New Spain (which was initially seen as a windfall) reflects a transition in perception from the sense of the colony as full of promise to a significant liability. This changing fate is reflected in a number of letters and statements from the era, none more incisive or characteristic than this example from Flemish scholar Justus Lipsius (1547-1606): "Conquered by you, the New World has conquered you in turn, and has weakened and exhausted your ancient vigor."[40] Similarly,

> [t]he Count-Duke of Olivares himself said at a meeting of the Council of State in 1631: "If its great conquests have reduced this Monarchy to such a miserable condition, one can reasonably say that it would have been more powerful without that New World."[41]

Thus Spain's home economics had significantly soured by Sor Juana's time, and the politics of the viceregal (colonial) court and the economic fragility of the Spanish state were constant sources of intrigue throughout her life.

The Spanish context as it confronted and formed Sor Juana was a potent mix of the triumphalism generated by the *Reconquista* and the promise (and reversal of that promise) of financial and spiritual riches harvested from a distant utopia. The images from the Americas that returned to Spain through the stories of the *Conquistadores* fed the imaginations of monarch and privateer alike. Financial potential was matched by the desire to add the Indigenous persons' souls to the roles of the Church. This led to an accelerated process of sending more *Conquistadores* and twelve Franciscan missionaries who followed Cortés in 1524.[42] And while the first steps of the conquest were bathed in optimism and hope, reports of brutality and exploitation quickly led to controversy.

Religious entrepreneurship mirrored the way that economic realities developed. The Church's representatives—the twelve Franciscans, initially—apparently sincerely valued the opportunity to meet with and preach to the Indigenous inhabitants of Mesoamerica. The missionaries sent were initially afforded great leeway in their efforts. That freedom was quickly curtailed.[43] Unfortunately for the Church, the temporal and spiritual conquests were quickly conflated:[44]

> In return for Spain's undertaking to evangelize American

> natives, Rome gave the crown control over the tithes, the right to nominate candidates for church offices at all levels, regulation of movement of clergy across the Atlantic, and veto powers over papal dispatches to America...all this made the colonial church an arm of the state.[45]

The institution of the *patronato real* or "royal patronage" effectively combined state and Church power within the monarchy: "...[*patronato real*] meant that the kings [and the queen] had the right to nominate—and therefore practically to appoint—bishops and other high ecclesiastical officers for the New World. With few exceptions, the crown was also able to administer tithes and other offerings, and to be responsible for all the expenses of the church. The result was that the church in Spanish America had very few direct dealings with Rome, and became practically a national church under the leadership of the Spanish kings and their appointees."[46]

By the middle of the sixteenth century, substantial debates—theological, political, anthropological—had come to attend any discussion of the "new" world.[47] Economic problems, exacerbated by numerous wars and battles throughout Europe, compelled the Spanish monarchs to a policy of aggressive exploitation of the wealth of the Indies. On the religious side, the vision of a new Eden and a "place" for utopia—coupled with the ideal of Christian *limpieza de sangre*—led to increasingly suspect evangelistic strategies.

The *Reconquista*, the material and spiritual conquest of the Americas, and the subsequent systemization of the colonizing process all had (and have) profound effects on the formation of the Spanish culture which influenced Sor Juana. Sor Juana's cultural milieu was formed through forces unleashed in the re-conquest of Spain, the emphasis on *limpieza de sangre* and orthodoxy, the complex and brutally effective bureaucracy that surrounded her, and the financial desperation that led Spain to ignore human rights in favor of productivity.

## Encomienda, Hacienda, and Convent

These general political and economic features of Spain were expressed in specific forms and institutions. Sor Juana's individual voice was further influenced by the communal voices of the institutions that surrounded her. There were many, of course, but those with the most direct impact were those that governed her financial options, those that shaped the racial and ethnic forces around her, and those that affected the relationship of Spain with New Spain. These institutions variously gave Sor Juana her context, her vocabulary, and the conversations she listened to and eventually joined.

Part of what is fascinating about Sor Juana is the way that she related to these various political, cultural, and religious institutions that surrounded her. She deftly managed a challenge which all individuals must navigate: who am I in relation to others? She was perceptive enough to see how institutions could benefit her, but her work was not without critique of these same institutions. Her writing criticizes assumptions about many aspects of life—such as when in a famous poem she condemns "foolish men" for making assumptions about gender roles. And she was constantly playing with the boundaries around religious discourse, too, letting the force of her artistic expressions bump up against the religious sensibilities approved by the Church. To see how Sor Juana interacted with institutions in more detail, it is worth exploring three key instances: the *encomienda*, the *hacienda*, and the convent.

### *The Encomienda and Hacienda*

To ensure the productivity of the patronage system as it was used in the colonization process, and allegedly to ensure the evangelization of the Indigenous peoples, the so-called *encomiendas* included the transfer of people along with the transfer of land.[48] The lords in charge of each *encomienda* were charged with the care of the

Indigenous persons, though in practice this was often neglected or reversed completely, and exploitation and abuse was common. The *encomiendas* centralized power around the *Conquistador*, whose influence radiated out from the center of the lands under his control. The land and the people within those boundaries were his "reward" for the financial and personal risks which accompanied exploration. Over time, this centralized form of organizing and ruling people and land developed into the *hacienda*, a reworking of the same basic institution. The *hacienda* was essentially a large house or group of houses occupied by the custodian of the property. The owner may or may not have been involved in the first waves of exploration and appropriation of land. As with the *encomienda,* the power radiated out from the house and included the land and the people within its boundaries.

This institution mirrored a similar situation in Spain, and for many of the same reasons: like Spain, especially the areas around Extremadura and Granada, New Spain had a dearth of irrigated land and was especially difficult to develop for agriculture.[49] The Indigenous people continued to farm maize according to their own well-developed practices, and therefore they were not potential clients for any agricultural production from the *haciendas.* Rather, they provided the labor, and Spain itself provided the demand for their products. Aside from grains needed to feed the stock animals on the *haciendas,* the market for agricultural goods in New Spain itself was extremely limited. Raw materials and a limited number of agricultural products were therefore exchanged with Spain, but perhaps only as often as once a year when shipping channels and escort boats could be provided to protect the fleets from the constant threat of piracy.

The *hacienda* developed around the economic and practical forces at work in the colony of New Spain, but importantly it also mirrored the cultural realities of the colonizing culture. Similar (basically feudal) arrangements predated the period of intense colonization of Mesoamerica in Spain. As a common feature of the Spanish landscape and cultural milieu, these *haciendas* or feudal centers organized power around a central individual or family. And while the institution clearly reduced the freedoms of those providing the labor, the benefits to the inhabitants of this arrangement were significant. Persons inside the hacienda—from lords to workers—were provided military protection and the ability to escape the agricultural cycle of feast and famine that was typical of Spain and Mesoamerica. With similar meteorological patterns in Mexico/New Spain, the *hacienda* provided a consistent source of protection against the frequent droughts and years of little or no agricultural production.[50] The centralized nature of the *hacienda,* and its tremendous ability to stockpile resources (generated by the very infrequent chances for shipping to Spain), provided a measure of year-to-year stability in terms of access to food. Also, and similar to the situation in Spain itself, the *hacienda* provided a degree of protection—both from other Spanish colonizers and from groups bent on violence for other reasons.

A further aspect of the development of the *hacienda* likewise mirrors the experiences of Spain and transfers them to the colonial context: depopulation. The Spanish experienced massive depopulation at various times during the decades and centuries prior to their intense phase of colonization, especially during the sixteenth-century plagues and famines and then (particularly in urban centers) following the expulsion of the Jews in 1492. In response to this depopulation (and its negative effect on production and economic vitality), Spain developed new centrally-located feudal sites through granting land and towns to lords. In New Spain, the microbial shock and violence against the Indigenous peoples led to massive depopulation, though in this case the response differed substantially: African slaves were imported by Spain to the colony to replace the labor lost by Indigenous depopulation.

In addition to its moral bankruptcy, the African slave trade was linked to the further tragedy of the loss of huge swaths of the Mesoamerican population. *Haciendas* required tremendous amounts of labor, as did the many silver, gold, mercury, and lead mines that were developed to feed Spain's need for raw materials and financing for its wars and court. African slaves were the horrific solution to this labor crisis, further increasing the cultural complexity of the colony of New Spain and the moral absurdities that would eventually lead to resistance, protest, and rebellion.

Though formed as a response to economic factors and basically able to address many financial needs in Spain, there were many negative aspects of the patronage system and its development into the *hacienda* and (later) a mine-based economy. One of these unforeseen developments was competition in the market: New Spain eventually developed the capacity to produce more than just raw materials, and the *obrajes* or "factories"—though not highly industrialized—became capable of finishing many of the raw materials that New Spain had previously shipped to Spain in their natural form.[51] The importation of silk worms into New Spain, and the finishing of that silk and its shipment back to Spain, is an instance of the ability of some entrepreneurs to capitalize on the availability of slave labor and lack of competition in the colony.[52] Spanish merchants, angered by developments such as these, lobbied the monarchs for protection—and soon the practice of "finishing" products in the colonies was either prohibited or heavily taxed. This attempt to control and suppress market forces, and the unintended consequences of the economic development of factory-like *obrajes* in New Spain, illustrates one of the negative aspects of the patronage system: it depended too heavily on external controls and protectionism, thereby stifling development and entrepreneurship.[53]

The religious aspects of the *encomienda* and *hacienda* also fall into positive and negative categories. On the one hand, the centralized control of this institution allowed a certain degree of vigilance and influence, fostering homogeneity in both culture and religious practice. On the other hand, the fact is that most lords of *haciendas* or *encomiendas* were little concerned with religious matters, focusing more on capacities for production and development. Thus the religious aspect of their assigned responsibility for the catechesis and religious development of the people commended to them often languished. The response to this challenge came frequently in yet another version of the centralized and bordered institution of catechetical schools (largely founded and run by Jesuits) which took religious education as a priority. Such schools looked very similar to *haciendas*—though without the massive wealth and without the same economic concern. These schools were not long tolerated, however, and flourished primarily (and briefly) in the earlier phases of evangelization of Mesoamerica (1524-1555).[54] After the middle of the sixteenth century, increasing Church control and proscription led to suspicion of the autonomous schools and their disbanding.[55]

Sor Juana was affected by the centralizing tendencies of the patronage system in a variety of ways. Her late adolescence and early adulthood was spent as part of the viceregal court, the extension of Spanish royalty into the colonial environment. As a participant in this viceregal system, she was affected by its nature (similar to the *hacienda*) as a distant "vision" of the centralized power of the colonizing force: "[t]he court in Mexico as a reflection of the court in Madrid was supposed to suggest the glitter and power of the far-off ruler."[56] The cultural, economic, literary, and religious aspects of the viceregal court oriented her toward Spain and allowed her to understand the position of one depending on a distant and centralized organizing principle.

### *The Convent*

Just as economic forces created the pressure needed to develop the *encomienda* and the *hacienda*, so too did religious and cultural pressures lead to the development of the centralized and highly-defined institution of the convent.[57] As colonization of New Spain developed, the ruling class became concerned that their daughters had difficulty finding appropriate opportunities for marriage.[58] In the highly stratified cultural environment, marrying "below" one's family position was prohibited. Dowries demanded by the families of potential mates were extremely high.

This scarcity of opportunities for strategic marriages was joined by the religious rhetoric of the era. This rhetoric was dominated by assumptions about gender roles. The male gaze and associated beliefs about the "fragility" of women led to the transplantation of the well-developed Spanish institution of the convent.[59] Modeled on the monastic formula, the convent answered the two primary concerns of suitable marriage and the need to "protect" women from the vagaries of life. Moreover, religious and cultural rhetoric of the time suggested that women needed to be isolated from men for the sake of the males' own moral and religious good. The institution of the convent allowed the isolation of women, at once protecting them as well as "protecting" men from their tempting presence. It is wrong to assume cynically that valid and sincere religious devotion was missing from the development of the convents. It is clear, however, that in addition to religious motivations, misogyny and oppressive gender roles played a significant part. The institution of the convent, like that of the *encomienda* and the *hacienda*, reflects the power of the patron—religious or economic—to influence large populations within a well-defined enclave.

Sor Juana was affected personally by the viceregal court and the convent of Saint Paula where she lived. Some of this influence can be detected in her work. She tangentially addressed the patronage systems that were a common part of life in New Spain. Her secular play *Los empeños de una casa* or "The Trials of a (Noble) House" explores the cultural realties of the Spaniards and the Criollos (children of Spaniards who were born in the colony) living in New Spain. It centers on relationships with the servant class and the culture which created it.[60] New Spain's population was divided into a dizzying array of racial categories, and *Los empeños* uses the drama of finding an appropriate mate within these categories as the primary way of naming and investigating them. The play is permeated with humor, puns, double meanings, and teasing, but it also displays through the institution of marriage the absurdities of the multivalent class structure and the way that these class structures circumscribed the rituals of life.

Apart from her critiques, however, it remains true that Sor Juana's literary production was enabled through the patronage systems deployed by Spain in its colonies. She was, first of all, a Criolla, and while not at the pinnacle of the class system, was still privileged. Moreover, she had access to the court through the viceregal system, and her early writing was made possible by her relative leisure and the availability of ready-made poetic forms and a ready-made audience. In her transition to convent life, Sor Juana gave up various perquisites of the courtly world, trading them instead for those peculiar to convent life. Her life at the convent of St. Paula was, according to most accounts, fairly unencumbered by work and obligations. She was able to collect a substantial library and was able to receive visitors. She had a servant girl. She helped teach in the girls' school associated with the convent, writing lyrics for some of their plays and productions. Beyond this, her life was largely devoted to learning and writing.

And although there were many privations associated with convent life, and although the patriarchal nature of the culture left her in a vulnerable and supervised position, she ultimately was able to pursue her vocation as writer *because* of a system of patronage. Most convents were founded by wealthy benefactors (women and men, interestingly) and maintained by private donations and patronage. While the convent system and associated systems of centralized control were imperfect and vulnerable to abuses, it must also be realized that the women inhabiting convents exercised a great deal of individual and collective agency. They discovered ways to subvert the patriarchal forces which may ostensibly have led them to their professions. Their religious devotion, as well as their ability to order their daily lives to a large degree on their own terms, led to a productive institution which fostered the creativity of Sor Juana and many like her. Though she is widely known, she is not unique. Convents and other forms of patronage, each reflections of familiar institutions in the parent culture of Spain, became symbols of Spanish power in New Spain/Mexico—but they were also shaped by their inhabitants in unexpected ways, as the work of Sor Juana demonstrates.

# Chapter 2

# Religious, Literary, and Intellectual Trends in Spain

*Sor Juana was a nun and a poet, devoted to theology and mythology, inquisitive about the sciences, a music lover, and a gatherer of unusual information... A nun by profession but a poet by birth; we must therefore begin with poetry and literature. In the forefront are the Spanish poets of the sixteenth and seventeenth centuries who formed her tastes, guided and inspired her.*[61]

## Sor Juana's Voice

Sor Juana wrote within and around genres. She at once conformed to the literary fashions prevalent during her writing career and frequently managed to transcend them. The genres she engaged in and expanded are (with the exception of her epistolary writing) largely out of fashion today. We are unlikely, for example, to read a *loa, villancico,* or *auto sacramental.* Each of these genres had currency within Sor Juana's time, however, and many writers were determined to be the best at one or several of them. Writers competed openly amongst each other. Whereas writers today might measure "likes" or page views, Sor Juana's contemporaries vied to outdo each other within the strictures of a well-defined literary convention. Syllable counts, subject matter restrictions, and manners of addressing the audience were only a few of the variables of any given genre which challenged the writer who wished to compete.

## Spanish Mysticism

It is tempting to place Sor Juana's work within the flow of Spanish Mysticism. There are similarities, but the differences are substantial. Two of the most effective and well-known examples of writers in this vein are Santa Teresa de Ávila (1515-1582) and San Juan de la Cruz (1542-1591). This strain of religious writing was a development of the Catholic Reformation, ever so slightly predating the Protestant Reformation, and focusing especially on reforming the internal structures of the Roman Catholic Church.[62] Santa Teresa shared Queen Isabella's earlier concern with restoring the institution of the monastery. Santa Teresa's Discalced[63] Carmelite monastic reforms accomplished much by way of improving the general moral standards of the monastic institution.[64] In addition to her accomplishments as a reformer, and clearly related to them, Santa Teresa's primary gift was her ability as a writer and poet. She perceived an obsession with material wealth within the Church. Part of her effort to remove the burden of avarice from the church is reflected in her spiritual practice and writing. She sought to detach herself from the material world and to "ascend" to a place of spiritual union with God. She began with herself, then, as an individual example of the needed corporate reforms. The methodology and techniques outlined by Ignatius Loyola (1491-1556), and Ignatian spirituality in general, helped her to build a spiritual practice that was rigorously oriented toward the divine and suspicious of material comfort and wealth.[65] As such, her writing as much as her reform—through the example of her spiritual practice—worked against the grain of corruption and corpulence which plagued the Church in the latter half of the sixteenth century. By emphasizing the goal of mystical union with

God and shunning the acquisition of wealth and comfort, Santa Teresa worked to effect positive change in the Church.

Similarly, fellow reformer (and fellow Carmelite) Juan de la Cruz valued "union with God" above all other objects of spiritual pursuit.[66] Well-read and astute, Juan de la Cruz also worked to break down the barriers between spiritual practice and the academic understanding of religion, ultimately favoring the mystical mode over the scholarly. And while he wrote comparatively little, his *Dark Night of the Soul* is among the great accomplishments of Spanish literature. The work features a spiritual or mystical reunion with God using the metaphor of a bride (the soul) united with the groom (Christ/God).[67] The use of this metaphor, and its eventual culmination in union with God, exemplifies one of the key contributions of Spanish mysticism: it uses artistic and poetic ways of knowing to learn and communicate truths about the nature of God and the soul. Not content to know God merely through academic, liturgical, or propositional means, Juan de la Cruz places the journey of the soul at the center of the search for knowledge of the divine. An epistemological prioritization of the mystical mode is a departure from previous ways of knowing. It demonstrates suspicion of the intellect and trust in the abilities of the soul to know its creator and source, and its far-reaching influence certainly had much to do with Sor Juana's work.

Santa Teresa and San Juan de la Cruz shared similar concerns for the reform of the Church. Their collaboration has been widely celebrated.[68] The Carmelite orders of each were based on monastic models from wide-ranging parts of Europe (including as far away as England) but ultimately were based on the model of the Desert Fathers and Mothers. The rule of the Carmelite orders emphasized physical privation coupled with spiritual discipline. Solitude, spiritual friendship (which the two shared), consistent practice, and a basic trust of the soul's ability to know God are hallmarks of their work. In pursuing these goals with these methods, each contributed vastly to the development of the Church in Spain, and each in their way prepared a mode of discourse which led to a peculiar *freedom of speech*. Even surrounded by the Spanish Inquisition[69], especially charged with monitoring the orthodoxy of religious utterances and particularly focused on the *Conversos* (Jews who converted to Christianity) and *Moriscos* (Muslims who converted to Christianity), Santa Teresa and San Juan de la Cruz were able to employ the "safe" mode of discourse developed to express mystical truths.[70] The employment of metaphor, dreamscape, imaginative constructs of every kind, and allegorical representations of various religious elements allowed the mystics to write with a freedom not afforded those whose more discursive works might attract scrutiny or censorship.

The successes of these two mystics—their widening audiences and influence over the piety of the moment—dovetailed effectively with the evolving response to Protestantism and the Counter-Reformation. This furthered the Church's self-assessment and defense in light of the critiques of the Protestant Reformers.[71] As examples of devotion, piety, and moral purity, mystics like Santa Teresa and San Juan de la Cruz were well-positioned to participate in the series of reforms and soul-searching of the Counter-Reformation.

Almost a century later, Sor Juana benefited from the mystical paths broken by Santa Teresa de Ávila and San Juan de la Cruz. Sor Juana mentions Santa Teresa infrequently, but when she does it is with affection and reverence: in *La Respuesta a Sor Filotea,* for example, Sor Juana calls Teresa "[t]he holy mother, my mother, Teresa."[72] But this benefit was related more to her ability to write and to be heard than it was to the epistemological influence of the mystics.[73] Like Santa Teresa and San Juan, of course, Sor Juana wrote as a member of a religious order—though she had quickly changed from a "discalced" or "unshod" convent to the more luxurious "calced" Hieronomite (under the patronage of Saint Jerome) convent of San Paula.[74] Nevertheless, the similarities are significant, and the lineage shared by Sor Juana and Santa Teresa is occasionally made explicit, as in *La Respuesta a Sor Filotea.*[75] Obviously, too, Sor Juana had in common with Santa Teresa the fact that she was a woman monastic writing about religious subjects. Nuns in convents in New Spain, especially in the mid- to late seventeenth century, were encouraged (sometimes required) to write about their religious experiences for the edification of themselves and others.[76]

The similarities begin to break down here, however, since Sor Juana was in her poetry and drama loath to write specifically about *her own* religious experience. A number of readers of Sor Juana have commented on her discontinuity with the Spanish mystical tradition, even while acknowledging its undeniable influence.[77] José Antonio Maravall, for example, stridently identifies this distinction between mysticism and the baroque:

> Spanish mysticism was a short-lived and delimited phenomenon, and nothing remained of it in the seventeenth century...the aspects characterizing mysticism, at least as it occurred in Spain (with St. Teresa and St. John of the Cross) were straightforwardly different from those of the baroque; they were rather anti-Baroque.[78]

Specifically, then, whereas Santa Teresa explored the "Interior Castle" of her own religious experience and wrote beautifully about the soul's attempt to find union with God, Sor Juana's poetry reflected largely courtly themes (early on) and later (during her convent years) acts of devotion either to God or to her friends and patrons. Her subjective religious experience is hidden or avoided. We learn more about her personal beliefs, emotions, and allegiances from her later epistolary prose than we do from her poetry and drama.

An apparent exception to this is her most famous long poem, the 975-line *Primero Sueño* ("First Dream" or, translated idiosyncratically by Margaret Sayers Peden, "First I Dream").[79] In her *Respuesta a Sor Filotea,* Sor Juana claims that "I cannot recall having written anything for my own pleasure except a little scrap of a thing they call *El Sueño*."[80] Affected humility aside (a "little scrap" hardly describes this long poem), this statement of Sor Juana's indicates the privileged status that the *Sueño* enjoys among her works. The *Sueño* shares a number of tropes with the poetry of the mystics, primarily the notion of the soul's journey into a place of special knowledge through a dream. While the Spanish mystics employed the vehicle of the dream to demonstrate their ascent into a place of special knowing, however, Sor Juana's *Sueño* is concerned more with epistemological questions and the philosophical means of knowing *per se*. It is less concerned with union with the divine.[81] Sor Juana's *Sueño* begins with the soul's sleep, but quickly segues through a host of mythological allusions (owls from Egypt and eagles from Mesoamerica, just to name two) and similar conceits, all very much in keeping with the conceits of *Gongorismo* (a particular version of Baroque poetry which she admired). The dreaming soul ascertains a pyramid—another element of the fascination with Egyptology she learned especially from German Jesuit Athanasius Kircher (c. 1601-1680)[82]—and begins its ascent. Again, ostensible similarities with the mystical trope of the soul's ascent prove to be superficial. While the mystic's ascent results in union with God, Sor Juana's soul ascends and ultimately grows more and more "confused."[83] Knowledge multiplies, but so does complexity. The soul becomes frustrated with its inability to discern a solid foundation for knowledge. Mystical knowing is not attained, and union with God is not the object of the *Sueño*.

Ultimately, Sor Juana's use of the tropes of mysticism must be characterized more by her departure from them than by their similarities. The *Sueño* uses the image of the soul's dream and journey, but the goal differs substantially from the goals of most mystical writing prior to her work. And while the mystics placed their trust in the soul's ability to discern special (and unifying) knowledge of the divine, Sor Juana's epistemological poem ends in a kind of uncertainty in the face of multiple and imperfect ways of knowing. Divine union, the goal and the methodology of the mystics, is not something that Sor Juana appears to trust or to seek in the *Sueño*.

It is crucial, too, that Sor Juana's preference for the academic epistemology of her (male) theological peers places her in a riskier mode of discourse than Santa Teresa (or San Juan de la Cruz, for that matter) enjoyed. By charting a mystical way of knowing, and making her own internal experience her subject, Santa Teresa avoided coming into direct competition with the theological discourse of those empowered by the Church to speak authoritatively on theological subjects: ordained and educated males. Sor Juana spoke openly on these subjects, particularly later in her career. By eschewing a mystical epistemology and employing instead the academic epistemology of her male peers in theological discourse—especially in the *Carta Atenagórica*, but elsewhere as well—Sor Juana opened herself to reprimand. Had she in fact written more in the mystical mode and less in the theological, she might not have attracted the same level of negative attention that eventually led to controversy. Sor Juana was influenced by the mystical vision, then, but did not herself speak in a mystical voice.

## Word Puzzles and Polemics: Spanish Baroque Poetry and its influence on Sor Juana

If mysticism provides a general literary background and point of departure, the more specific literary fashions of Sor Juana's time provided the mold which gave her work its specific shape. Sor Juana's work was influenced more immediately by the Baroque artistic sensibility, in particular by the forms of Baroque literature known as "Gongorismo." This mode is named for the work of poet Luis Góngora y Argote (1561-1627).[84]

Góngora was a dominant force in Spanish letters during his career. He was not the only voice, however. It is impossible to appreciate his style without exploring his writing in contrast with his poetic and philosophical foil, Francisco Quevedo (1580-1645). Both were pioneers of Baroque literary forms of the latter part of the seventeenth century, but these two poets were partisans of different schools of the general Baroque sensibility.

Spanish Baroque poetry was characterized by its delight in ornamentation and its appropriation of symbols from widely disparate cultures and epochs. Spanish Baroque poetry was also virtually unique in its ability to encode knowledge and insight within intricately wrought conceits and tropes. Their techniques engage the reader in a seemingly endless series of allusion and incorporation of unexpected myths and legends. It occasionally seems that Spanish Baroque literary constructions appear to have more in common with games and puzzles than they do with pure expression. References come from all sorts of sources, but the subjects and theses are seldom named explicitly. This could be related to the environment created by the Inquisition: the ability to encode (and thus to hide) one's true thoughts and feelings behind multiple linguistic hedges was especially valuable in a censorious world.

The Baroque is not obscurantist, however, though it may risk this. Scholars of Baroque literature see the codes employed as reflections of a particular perception of reality, a sort of mimetic blur of words that mirrors the complexity of the world as apprehended by the senses. Far from being mere pyrotechnics, then,

> ...it is more accurate to identify Gongorism with erudition; elegance; wit; and stylish, polished artifice. The poet saturates the text with rhetorical figures, heaps elaborate conceit upon elaborate conceit, contorts syntax with hyperbata, interrupts narrative flow with ellipses, and bombards his audience nonstop with synesthetic effects and allusions to classical myth.[85]

The multi-ethnic and multicultural landscape of Spain in the seventeenth century, in conversation with the so-called Renaissance developing more broadly in Europe, combined in the Baroque poets to produce a veritable festival of wide-flung images, tropes, conceits, and literary inventions. It is dizzying in its complexity. When well done, though, it is uniquely satisfying, incisive, and provocative. Carlos Fuentes sees the proliferation of visual symbols related to Spain's multi-religious heritage—Muslim architecture not least among these, as well as elements of Christian material religion and Jewish religious practice—as part of the primordial soup which gave rise to the Baroque sensibility in literature.[86]

Góngora and Quevedo were masters of this form and stretched the Baroque sensibility to its limits. They were similar but distinct. Each inhabited this Baroque space differently: Góngora is classified as a proponent of *culteranismo,* while Quevedo is associated with *conceptismo.*[87] *Culteranismo,* for its part, is fascinated with the "cultured" aspects of language, obsessed with learning and peculiar terminologies. This rarified lexicon is paired with a torturously complex syntax, leading to lengthy sentences and maze-like constructions. On the other hand, *conceptismo*—more associated with Quevedo—delights in marvelously-wrought conceits, tropes, figures of speech, and extended metaphors.[88] Ideas—"concepts"—take priority over *le mote juste* and syntactical pyrotechnics. The perspective of history has tended to identify Góngora as the more influential of the two writers, and the literary style known as "Gongorismo" reflects his work and preferences. Nevertheless, these two sides of the Spanish Baroque coin are equally important for readers of Sor Juana: her own version of the Baroque style of poetic composition shows her to be equally masterful with each of these voices, whether in word choice, syntax, or the dazzling complexity of her figures of speech.

Other scholars have seen the way in which the Baroque sensibility travels from Spain into New Spain and becomes part of the expression of the multi-cultural and culturally hybridized New

Spanish/Mexican context.[89] Assimilating symbols and images from disparate sources—whether Egypt, Greece, Rome, wider Europe, past poets, and so on—Baroque poetry's omnivorous glance found a home for the scattered ideas and icons left by the many cultures which had occupied the Iberian Peninsula. Thus the Baroque poetic mode capitalized on the (perhaps) unarticulated need for Spain in the seventeenth century to discern how the pieces of its motley history fit together. Given a basket of seemingly unrelated images and themes, the Baroque poets were able to craft something with its own internal logic and integrity. The influence of the mother country (Spain) was such that its fashions were sometimes exaggerated in the colonial setting. This intensification of European modes of thinking and writing were pushed even further in the colonies—as if to insist that the parent culture was stronger than the culture(s) being colonized. Following this pattern, then, what was fashionable in Spain filtered into New Spain in an exaggerated form. The American version of Baroque literature is sometimes called *Barocco de las Indias* or "the Baroque of the Indies."[90] Octavio Paz, commenting on the exaggerated form of Baroque poetry in the Americas, points out that the "excesses" of the *Barocco de las Indias* are "proof" of its "authenticity": transplanted across the Atlantic, the already-dramatic figures of the Spanish Baroque are brought into the American sphere with even more flourish and flair.[91]

Sor Juana proved to be unusually expert at exploiting the sensibilities of the Spanish Baroque literary style. Her own natural love of learning and the fact that she was self-taught and able to read in any direction her interests led her, created a body of knowledge made up of elements from every conceivable cultural and historical corner. She was fascinated with cooking, music, science, mythology, mathematics, languages, biology, and nature in general—not to mention the Bible and Christian theology. Her deep admiration and knowledge of the work of German Jesuit Athanasius Kircher fueled her interest in Egyptology and the empirical sciences as well as the idea of the encyclopedia. Kircher was famous for inventing or "discovering" the "magic lantern," an early version of the movie projector capable of projecting an image onto an adjacent wall. He wrote extensively on magnetism and studied classics of philosophy, architecture, and so on. The polymath, then, was an appropriate type for Sor Juana to adopt—and it dovetailed perfectly with the Baroque poetic love of all things exotic and unfamiliar.

Not all of Sor Juana's works are equally reflective of these tendencies. But some fit the pattern especially well. For example, her *Primero Sueño* is perhaps the best example of this hunger for unusual images and their assembly into a surprisingly coherent poetic work. The opening scenes of the poem are a veritable grotesquerie. They combine elements of Egyptian mythology and Mesoamerican symbols with obscure allusions and incredibly complex syntax. Clauses are nested one within the next and then subsequently attached to their antecedents. The meaning of the poem cannot be accessed until (and unless!) the challenges of the syntactical game are overcome.

Another important aspect of the Baroque with significance for Sor Juana is its ability to encode multiple meanings. Given the censorious presence of the Spanish Inquisition, and given its presence in New Spain from about the middle of the 1500's, Sor Juana (along with others) was highly motivated to express herself in writing in ways that could be interpreted variously.[92] While propositional theological statements came later in life for her (and caused her trouble), her equally theologically significant poetry was unchallenged and even celebrated by religious authorities. She was able, it seems, to use the multiple masks of the Baroque poetic sensibility to cover any overtly theological freight in her works. Even if challenged, a poem written in the Baroque mode could not easily be pinned down to one particular meaning—and this added yet another element of protection.

The breakthroughs in Spanish literature related to the work

of Góngora and Quevedo led to a widely imitated style. Their success and fame was due not only to their stunning skill, but also to their ability to read their culture and to discern a way to assemble disparate elements of Spanish narrative elements—its tri-religious heritage, its history of multiple races and cultures living in alternating harmony and acrimony, its regionalism. To this Spanish cultural mix they were able to add the vast products of the Renaissance, the fascination with classical learning, with visual art, with the possibilities of knowing in an encyclopedic way. And they were able, using the allusive and complex forms they preferred, to maintain great notoriety without Church and state censorship—though Góngora did eventually serve jail time for his mockery of government inefficiencies.

Sor Juana's use of the Baroque poetic genre built on the accomplishments of Góngora, Quevedo, Lope de Vega, and others, magnifying their flourishes and yet becoming (by some critical accounts) even more expert in these literary forms then the Spaniards. The *Barocco de Indias*—this exaggerated form of the Baroque—becomes in time a durable element of the Mexican sensibility, visible for decades in the constant use of ornamentation in poetry, architecture, popular and material religion—all of them ornamented and visually complex in their iconography.

Finally, the aspect of competitiveness among poets had an influence on Sor Juana. To the extent that poets such as Góngora and Quevedo competed in their poetic careers, they thereby developed specific poetic forms—with designated rhyme schemes, syllabic strictures, and so on—and jousted to see who could fulfill the form most effectively. These competitive poetic forms made their way to New Spain—and Sor Juana proved herself a master at them. She wrote a number of poems to fit peculiar formats, frequently excelling and wining wide praise in Spain and in Mexico.[93] Her accomplishments in this mode, as well as her more general poetic and literary accomplishments within the Baroque genres, led to the final volume of her works (published posthumously in

Spain in 1700) to sport the title *Fama y obras póstumas de la poetisa Sor Juana Inés de la Cruz, la decima musa, la Fénix de Mexico,* and so on: Sor Juana is named "the Tenth Muse" and "the Mexican Phoenix." Baroque hyperbole aside, these honorifics signify the unusually high level of fame and notoriety that she achieved in Spain itself—as revered as Góngora and Quevedo, though certainly not protected by this fame. The Baroque literary forms fit Sor Juana perfectly, and she both advanced the forms and made them her own from her convent in New Spain.

## Philosophical Influences: The Debate at Valladolid, 1550-1551

Poetic sensibilities were not the only intellectual influences on Sor Juana's work. A discussion around the proper treatment of the Indigenous Peoples of Spain's colonies had been ebbing and flowing throughout the Church and society ever since Isabella's 1503 letter instituting the *encomienda.*[94] A number of the streams of thought which developed over the decades after the initial "discovery" of the Americas came to a head at a debate held in the Spanish town of Valladolid during 1550-1551. Called by Charles V during a temporary halt to expansion in the colonies, this debate revolved around the reading of prepared texts which represented each of the sides. Though the debate was inconclusive, it is a clear instance of the philosophical and theological streams of thought which would have been very familiar to Sor Juana.[95]

By the time Bartolomé de las Casas (1484-1566) arrived in New Spain, the institution of the *encomienda* was well-established.[96] The *encomienda* was developed as a way of rewarding the *Conquistadores* who risked their own private funds and resources to exploit the wealth of the new world on behalf of the Spanish monarchs. In exchange for making their risky journeys and developing the Americas as places of production of raw materials, the *Conquistadores* were given tracts of land as well as

Indigenous subjects to work and develop that land. Theoretically, the Indigenous persons were free, insofar as they could not be sold or otherwise detained, and the land-owners were obliged to educate and catechize their subjects. In practice, however, the *encomienda*s were essentially institutionalized slavery, rife with abuses and exploitation. Though the institution of the *encomienda* was designed to prevent abuses and to further the economic and religious development of the new world, the inherently dehumanizing nature of the institution showed itself almost immediately. The absurdity of *giving* human beings into the care of exploitative lords (the *Conquistadores* and their inheritors) angered de las Casas, and he returned to Spain with evidence and anecdotes to support his claims of the inhumanity of the *encomienda*s in New Spain/Mexico.

De las Casas vigorously attacked the institution of the *encomienda* and its promulgators, reporting to the Spanish crown the widespread misapplication of the model and the several abuses rampant in the colony of New Spain. Naturally, his descriptions included stories of the *Conquistadores* who were running these institutions—and his descriptions were far from flattering. His rhetorical abilities led him to draw attention to the sharp contrast between the idea of the *encomienda* and the practice of exploitation that he witnessed. In the process of painting this picture, he naturally offended those with interests in the continuation of the *encomienda*—both economic and religious.

The conflict of the various interests involved in the conquest—the religious concern for evangelization as much as the economic concern for development—led ultimately to the debate in Valladolid in 1550-1551. The debate included two major contenders—as well as a third (more moderate) position.[97] De las Casas advocated for the respectful and humane treatment of the Indigenous peoples, and the improvement of or elimination of the institution of the *encomienda*. Opposing this perspective was Juan Ginés de Sepúlveda (1489-1573)[98], whose position depended on his contention that the Indigenous people were "natural slaves."[99] This "natural" state of slavery and immaturity, he argued, enjoined upon the Spanish the *obligation* to order Indigenous persons' lives for their own good. Arguing from Aristotelian categories based on the "hierarchy of being," de Sepúlveda proposed that the Spanish practice of catechizing and employing the Indigenous people was ultimately beneficial and essentially rescued them from their state of natural slavery. Alex García-Rivera sees in this and related arguments a distinctly *anthropological* element heretofore un-emphasized, and points out that the backbone of de Sepúlveda's arguments is his contention that the Indigenous occupants of Mesoamerica were not in fact human in the same sense that the Spaniards were. There can be no such thing as humane treatment of an inhuman subject, and therefore the Spanish use of the *encomienda* was justified.

Far from supporting the cruelty of the *Conquistadores*, however, de Sepúlveda (profoundly influenced by the insights of Humanism) wished primarily to defend the philosophical underpinnings of the institution of the *encomienda.* He was not, as perhaps de las Casas' polemical rhetoric claimed, in favor of abject cruelty.[100] Nonetheless, de Sepúlveda's net contribution to the debate at Valladolid was to justify the *encomienda* and to argue for its continuation.

De las Casas, who had in fact seen the situation on the ground in the Caribbean and in New Spain, argued not against the ideal form of the *encomienda* but rather against the brutal nature of its realization in the colonies. The foundation of his argument was, like de Sepúlveda's, anthropological. De las Casas argued that the Indigenous people were just as human as the Spaniards who dominated them and therefore needed to be treated humanely. Apparent differences between the Indigenous people and the Europeans were trumped by the many similarities. While de Sepúlveda would argue that the Indigenous peoples had no cities and made no laws, de las Casas would cite the highly organized religious, urban, and political structures of Tenochtitlan, demonstrating that the Indigenous people had in fact developed an advanced civilization—thus exempting them from the category of "natural slaves." Given that the Aristotelian categories used by de Sepúlveda depended on these accomplishments, de las Casas' argument is compelling. De las Casas developed his argument for the basic humanity of the Indigenous people and made it clear that they were obviously human and needed to be treated with compassion. Evangelization was appropriate, he believed, but not through violent means.

Between these extremes, García-Rivera and others (Davíd Carrasco in his Introduction to *Religions of Mesoamerica*) place the position of Francisco Vitoria (1483-1546).[101] This position was carried into the debate through the "unsolicited reflections of the Salamanca School," the school of thought initiated by Vitoria's teachings at the University of Salamanca.[102] While de Sepúlveda argued that the Mesoamerican tribes were "natural slaves," Vitoria's argument (extrapolated into the Valladolid debate after his death in 1546) used similar Aristotelian categories and posited a middle rung on the ladder or hierarchy of being: the natural child. Vitoria claimed that the Indigenous persons were human—but that they were perpetually immature and "minor" and could not govern their own religious and societal lives. Children (so went the analogy) need parents to direct and rule them until they reach something like maturity and self-rule. In the case of natural children, this maturity might never come—so while the Indigenous people for Vitoria were higher than natural slaves, they were still in need of the direction and (dubious) care of the Spanish.

The debate was related to the notion of *bellum justum* or "just war," a category developed by the Church and its political allies to discern ways in which violent means could be used against others, either for their conversion or for the defense of the faith.[103] A host of different situations could lead to a conflict being a just war, and Vitoria categorically defeated each possible argument.

In short, then, he theoretically subverted the Spanish justification of violence, but did little to undermine the basic tenets of the *encomienda.*

De las Casas has come to be known as the "defender of the Indians" due to his impassioned support of their humanity and dignity. In the process of arguing for this dignity, however, he employed polemical rhetoric which doubtless blurred the lines between the actual practice of the encomienda and the cases of exceptional cruelty and exploitation. What is clear, though, is that de las Casas witnessed and was moved by images of Spanish cruelty against the Mesoamericans, and that the injustices demanded remedy. His religious convictions were no less strong than the humanistic convictions of de Sepúlveda, though, and it is remarkable that these two individuals came to such jarringly disparate positions. According to García-Rivera and others, these two extremes were eventually sidelined by the more moderate position of Vitoria—the notion that the Amerindians were natural children who needed the care and nurture of their Spanish adults.

García-Rivera sees in this outcome, ironically, a minor improvement in the conditions in New Spain—and, unfortunately, justification for the enslavement of Africans. With the massive depopulation brought on by active genocide and microbial shock (which cause more deaths in the new world than any other factor), the encomiendas (whatever their moral status) became too small an institution for the development of production. Africans were placed in the category of "natural slaves" (or, at best, "natural children") and brought to New Spain to work in developing trade and production. The categories of humanity, honed during the Valladolid debate, thus played a role in the justification of the institution of slavery. When the Mesoamericans went up a category (from "natural slaves" to "natural children"), the Africans were, tragically, recruited to occupy the vacancy.

By the time Sor Juana was reaching her most productive years as a writer in central New Spain, the debate at Valladolid was distant in time but very present in its influence. The categories of humanity developed during Valladolid and similar debates had morphed into a labyrinthine system of categorizing the occupants of the new world. Based on percentages of various races, and factoring in the location of one's birth and lineage, persons were placed into any one of perhaps dozens of categories and sub-categories. Many permutations of these categories developed and were part of the cultural milieu in which Sor Juana was formed. Ilan Stavans calls this systemization part of a "racial craze":

> The Spaniards had encountered a strong Indigenous population and quickly established a system of castes. At the top of the ladder were the ruling *españoles,* Spanish settlers heading legal and financial institutions. Next came the *criollos,* American-born descendants of the Spaniards. They were followed by the part-European and part-native *mestizos,* and then by the *castizos,* whose heritage was *mestizo* and white. The *indios* followed, and at the bottom of the ladder were *mulattos, zambos,* and other ethnic mixtures of Indians and African slaves.[104]

Sor Juana's writings show evidence of her awareness of this hierarchy and, in turn, the enduring influence of these debates (as epitomized by Valladolid) on her thought.

Three notable examples demonstrate the way that Sor Juana engaged these categories of racial and cultural assignments: her famous *tocotines* or songs based on an Indigenous genre, her *Loa* for the *auto sacramental* (religious play) *El divino narciso*, and her *Respuesta a Sor Filotea.* In the first of these, the *tocotines,* Sor Juana employs and thereby dignifies a genre created by a racial category other than her own. Herself a Criolla, or a Spaniard born in the colony of New Spain, she chose to explore a form of short song developed by a class of humanity which existed a few steps down from her in the logic of the prevailing categories. Her *tocotines*—of which we know two, though doubtless others were written and lost—are written either in Spanish plus Nahuatl or, in the second case, entirely in Nahuatl. Sor Juana therefore takes on the linguistic persona of an ethnic category other than her own. By the time Sor Juana was writing her *tocotines*, she was already wildly popular as a poet and dramatist both in New Spain and in Spain itself. Her poetic gifts led to widespread admiration, and her engagement with native Mesoamerican forms of poetic discourse served to make Spanish audiences more aware of Mesoamerican culture. Whether Sor Juana had the right to appropriate the artistic categories of the Mesoamericans is perhaps another question, but in any event, the *tocotines* can be seen as a transgression of the rigidly assigned categories of human being which grew in part out of the debate at Valladolid.

Sor Juana's 1689 *Loa* to *El divino narciso* is an even more overt amplification of the dignity of the Mesoamerican Indigenous people and shares much with the general arguments promulgated by de las Casas. The genre of the *Loa* consisted of a short, highly allegorical drama which was used to introduce the themes of the longer play which followed. They were, however, frequently performed as stand-alone pieces. The *Loa* for *El divino narciso* takes as its subject an imagined encounter between representatives of Mesoamerican culture and representatives of Spanish/Iberian culture. Being an allegorical work, of course, the characters are highly stylized and are reified versions of different cultural characteristics of each culture. Mesoamerican culture has Occident and America as its main characters, while Spain is represented by Zeal and Religion. Lesser characters fill in some of the space between these representations. The *Loa* begins with the Mesoamerican characters engaged in song and dance as they celebrate the "great God of the Seeds," a reference to the Aztec god Huitzilopochtli—often represented as a figure constructed of seeds held together by blood. As the Indigenous persons continue their dance, the Spanish characters enter—and are almost immediately shocked by what they see.

As the encounter unfolds, the Amerindians in the play enter into a dialogue with the Spanish characters. The conversation includes the evangelical strategizing of the Spanish characters, the explanations of the meaning of the rite by the Mesoamericans, and a wide-ranging consideration of the Sacraments of Baptism and Eucharist. The Spaniards are especially exercised over the apparent similarities between two religious practices of the Mesoamericans and those of Christianity: bathing in pure water before religious rites and the consuming of the God of the Seeds at their festival. The corollaries with Baptism and Eucharist are overwhelming and, for the Spaniards, disturbing. Employing a familiar trope of the period, they see these similarities not as proof of their common search for truth but rather as devilish mimicry of the true Sacraments of the Church. The similarities are evidence that the devil has copied the Church's rites and used the facsimile to dupe the Mesoamericans. As the conversation unfolds and the Mesoamericans show little interest in giving up their practices in favor of the Christian religion, the Spanish characters barely restrain themselves from violence. The threat of violence, though, hangs over the entire play and is made more pointed by the very real history of violence in the evangelistic history of New Spain. In the end, however, the characters representing Spain relent and, almost absurdly, begin to join in the dance and song celebrating the "great God of the Seeds." Those motivated to convert the Mesoamericans to Christianity are themselves converted to the (momentary?) practice of the Indigenous religion. The play closes with the Spaniards dancing and thanking God (*which* God is unclear) for letting them meet the God of the Seeds.

Making this play even more remarkable is the clue within the latter part of the play that it (and/or *El divino narciso)* were to be performed in Madrid for Spanish audiences. Thus Sor Juana, the author, places her audaciously subversive play before the Spanish people whom she has represented embracing Indigenous religious practice. The extremely positive representation of Mesoamerican religious practice echoes the extremely positive anthropological assessment rendered by de las Casas during the debate at Valladolid. And while Sor Juana does not go so far as to quote de las Casas, her work clearly exists within the same trajectory which de las Casas initiated. The argument is simple: the Mesoamericans' religious practice is similar to the Christian religious practice (versions of Baptism and Eucharist are central), and this suggests not only a common humanity but also a common search for religious truth. It also suggests the unity of religious truth, insofar as each culture—working independently—discerned such similar rites.

A final example of Sor Juana's continuity with de las Casas may be found in her *Respuesta a Sor Filotea*. This prose work was written as a defense of her (and other women's) right to engage in theological discourse and to be educated in theological and philosophical matters. Up to 1690, Sor Juana was content to write mostly poetry, drama, short liturgical pieces, and commissioned works for civil/religious events. After her comments on a sermon by Portuguese Jesuit Antonio Vieira (1608-1697)—a celebrated preacher—were published and circulated by her bishop, she became increasingly controversial as one who had wrongly entered into the male-dominated discourse of theology and philosophy.[105] Her bishop and erstwhile defender appended to her comments his own response to her critique of Vieira's sermon—writing as Sor Filotea, a fellow nun—and chastised Sor Juana for reading too widely and neglecting the "book of Jesus Christ." Perhaps not a complete betrayal, this letter of Sor Filotea—coupled with her critique, called the *Carta Atenagórica* or "letter worthy of Athena" by her bishop—led to Sor Juana's most famous prose work, her *Respuesta a Sor Filotea* or "Reply to Sister Philotea."

The *Respuesta* categorically enumerates her basic right to studies and to theological discourse, making frequent use of the precise anthropological categories used so effectively by de las Casas at Valladolid. In this instance, however, rather than using her common humanity to argue for ethnic rights and humane treatment, Sor Juana uses the humanity that she shares with men to argue for the same sorts of privileges that men enjoy. If we are both fundamentally human, she asks, why do men have the ability to participate in theological discourse and women do not? The argument from similarity suggested by de las Casas works equally well for racial categories as is does for gender categories. Sor Juana argues that from her childhood she was possessed by the desire to learn and to read and to write, and that this charism (God-given gift) entitles her to the same basic rights to expression as it would if manifested in a male. The charism is essential, the gender is accidental.

Sor Juana is, then, the inheritor of the categories developed by de las Casas, and she deploys them in similar ways. Sor Juana's use of these categories, however, revolves primarily around questions of gender and its implications for just treatment, while de las Casas was clearly more focused on justice among persons of different racial status. Nevertheless, the significance of the debate at Valladolid resonates throughout the continued unfolding of American history, and Sor Juana is among those that have either directly or indirectly benefitted from the understandings that it generated. And while de las Casas cannot be said to have won the debate, his vigorous defense of the Amerindians and his use of the notion of a shared humanity have done much to develop the emerging understanding of the encounter between European and Mesoamerican cultures in New Spain.

In addition to the literary and philosophical streams of discourse that shaped Sor Juana's world, the economic, political, and cultural forces which constituted New Spain made an indelible impression. Within New Spain we find elements of Mesoamerican Indigenous culture and religion, thought, and material culture mixed into the economic and political power that drove the process of colonization.

## Cultural Expectations of Sor Juana: Representing New Spain to Spain

Sor Juana's work reflects and reflects on the cultural encounter between Spain and Mesoamerica. Even when she is not directly addressing this encounter, her work exists within the tensions which that encounter created. Her readers, too, were sensitive to these dynamics, and eventually came to understand her as a a writer lodged between cultures and writing within that interstitial space. This perception of Sor Juana and her work can be seen in a fascinating image of her that appears in the frontispiece to the 1700 edition of her works published in Spain under the title *Fama y obras póstumas de la ilustre poetisa Sor Juana Inés de la Cruz*. Although Sor Juana was by then deceased, the image on the frontispiece gives a sense of how her work was placed and read in Spain: the emblematic frontispiece shows Sor Juana in her nun's habit, holding a plumed pen as if preparing to write.[106] On one side of her is an image of an armored Spanish nobleman, clad in steel and sporting a jaunty feather in his helmet. On the other side of Sor Juana is an image of a Mesoamerican man, clad in a loincloth and other distinctive garb of an Amerindian. Sor Juana is pictured between these two representations, apparently in the process of writing about the encounter between these two cultures.

Although too fluid still to be called a genre, reflection on the Iberian/Mesoamerican cultural encounter was emerging simultaneously elsewhere in the literature of the moment. Ilan Stavans notes in his *Introduction* to an anthology of Sor Juana's works:

> Together with [Sor Juana's] friend and devotee Carlos Sigüenza y Góngora, Mexico's leading man of letters in the seventeenth century, who in 1668 wrote *Primavera indiana*, a long poem in honor of the Virgin of Guadalupe, Sor Juana was among the first to juxtapose Christianity and

> native pagan mythology and to reflect on the encounter between the two civilizations.[107]

It is notable, too, that the subtitle of the work in question, the third volume of her extraordinarily popular works to be published posthumously in Spain, includes the term "Mexican"—here referring to her as the "Mexican phoenix."[108] The phoenix, regenerating every 500 years from its own ashes, is here termed "Mexican" and associated with Sor Juana—she is not *Spain's* phoenix, not *New Spain's* phoenix, not the *Aztec* phoenix—but a distinctly Mexican phoenix, demonstrating the way in which cultural awareness of a "new" national and racial identity was being born from the ashes of the two previous cultures. The word "Mexico" derives from one of the tribes assimilated by the Aztec/Nahua nation, the Mexica, as the Aztecs consolidated power in the last century or so before the arrival of Cortés in 1519-1521. The use of this term in a publication in Spain represents a novel naming and re-framing of the land where Sor Juana was born and wrote.

Clearly, too, this image on the frontispiece indicates that Spanish audiences fully expected Sor Juana's writings to include elements of Spanish culture, as well as elements of Mesoamerican culture. The image at the front of the book *promises* as much. But while the frontispiece clearly gives equal status to each representation of culture, Sor Juana's works themselves tend to answer primarily to Spanish Baroque requirements and less to those associated with Mesoamerican culture. Scholars who seek the influences of Mesoamerican culture in Sor Juana's works are sometimes frustrated by the apparently limited degree to which she appropriates the elements of the culture of the Indigenous peoples. For example, among many *villancicos* composed for festivals of the Virgin Mary, Sor Juana does not write anything based on the Guadalupe event and cult which developed after 1531 and which was central to the religious life of central Mexico. She mentions *La Virgen de Guadalupe* only in Sonnet 206.[109] What's more, her *tocotines,* or Nahua songs/dances, written either completely in Nahuatl or in half-Spanish, half-Nahuatl, make up only a fraction of her works—two are extant, and there is no certain proof that she wrote more.

Even so, elements of Mesoamerican religious practice and symbolism work their way into her writing, though typically in an adapted or ambivalent way. The primary example of this apparent ambivalence is the image of the eagle in her *Primero Sueño.* Entering the scene about halfway through this long poem, the eagle becomes part of the richly textured symbolic tapestry that provides the background for the dreaming soul's search for knowledge. And while some scholars read this eagle as a reference to the eagle that led the wandering Aztecs to the site of their famed Tenochtitlan, others point out that the eagle has symbolic resonance in Egyptian and European culture, as well. It is unclear, then, whether this can safely be read as a use of Mesoamerican culture.

While Sor Juana's writings contain some limited use of Mesoamerican cultural artifacts, her worldview is perhaps more clearly a product of the mixing of cultures that surrounded her. A fascinating starting point for this might be found in the very name of her birthplace: San Miguel de Nepantla, with "Nepantla" being the Nahua word for "a place between."[110] Nepantla in the Mesoamerican religious understanding was a place between the world of the living and the world of the dead, a place where special knowledge resided and which could be visited in trances or through the familiars of spirit animals. Sor Juana in other places remarks on her love for "her native land," and it is extremely significant that she means *Mexico* rather than *Spain.* Many Criollos even a generation before her might as likely have meant "Spain" if asked what their native land was, and Sor Juana's own father was from the Basque region of northern Spain. For her to identify Mexico as her native land—and for those in Spain to identify her as the Mexican phoenix—is telling.

The work in which Sor Juana makes her clearest representation of Mesoamerican culture—though within the confines of an admittedly Spanish genre—is her *Loa* for *El divino narciso*. This short play opens on a scene of music and dancing and chanted poetry directed at the "God of the Seeds," whom we know to be Huitzilopochtli, a god highly revered by the Aztecs and with similar status to Quetzalcoatl. The music, poetry, and dancing associated with this Indigenous religious festival clearly depends on the Mesoamerican way of knowing called *flor y canto*, in which truth is sought and expressed through categories of beauty and the arts. It amounts to an endorsement of Mesoamerican culture and epistemology. Moreover, Sor Juana describes the representations of Mesoamerican culture—America and Occident—as physically beautiful, peaceful, wise, open, and trusting. Her portrayal of their festival and their devotion to their religious life suggests that she considers them to have a high level of religious understanding. And when the Mesoamerican characters begin to interact with the representations of Christian religion and Spanish culture, it is the Indigenous characters who demonstrate greater reserve, tact, and wisdom. They are peaceful in the face of the Spanish questioning of their rite and the increasingly threatening rhetoric which the Spanish and Christian characters try out in the efforts to convert the Mesoamericans to their way of worship.

And as the short play develops, it is the Indigenous characters who finally educate the Spanish and Christian characters, teaching them how to understand their rite and even incorporating them into their dance and song. It is a tremendous reversal of expectations. The evangelical spirit of the Spanish and Christian characters eventually gives way to their acceptance of the God of the Seeds.

Toward the end of this *Loa*, Sor Juana includes a brief passage which indicates that the play introduced (*El divino narciso*) is to be performed in Madrid, giving the sense that the interaction between the representations of Mesoamerican and Spanish cultures was written with Spain in mind. Naturally, the *Loa* would travel with it, attached as a sort of preface. The notion that this ultra-positive representation of Indigenous culture, coupled with a distinctly critical portrayal of the bellicose missionary strategies of the Spanish, clearly indicates the prophetic role that this *Loa* could potentially have in Spain. For one thing, Sor Juana was very popular in Spain. Additionally, the genre of writing and teaching in support of the Indigenous peoples and against their exploitation was by then well established, having been pioneered by sympathetic souls like Bartolomé de las Casas. Finally, too, the starkly drawn allegorical nature of the characters in the play—caricatures, really—point up the clear failings of the Spanish spiritual conquest and the devaluation of Indigenous culture.

## Representing Indigenous Religious Practices under the Gaze of the Inquisition

Part of the larger context which Sor Juana's prophetic *Loa* addresses is the attitude of the Roman Catholic Church toward vestiges of Indigenous religious practices. It is important to keep in mind that the Inquisition in Spain was primarily concerned with policing the religious lives and utterances of Jews and Muslims who converted to Christianity (for whatever reason, religious or social).[111] The viceregal court in New Spain was the center of power from which other smaller centers of power were projected into New Spain. The viceroy was a "vicar" of the Spanish Crown, answerable directly to the monarch(s) and charged with the ordering and developing of the colony.[112] Considering the conflation of Church power with state power in Spain in the preceding century, it is no surprise that the extension of economic power from the viceroyalty included the extension of Church power. The production of raw materials was paralleled by the production of Christian subjects in New Spain—the converted Indigenous people. And just as the *haciendas* exerted control over the production of wealth on behalf of Spain, so did the viceroyalty and Church authorities preside over the evangelization of the Indigenous peoples. In contrast to the situation in Spain, however, in New Spain the Holy Office of the Inquisition had jurisdiction over the Spanish colonists and *not* over the Indians themselves:

> The Holy Office of the Inquisition had been introduced in New Spain in 1571 to ensure orthodoxy in the practice of Catholic religion and to prosecute any breach in the observance of the sacraments...the Holy Office exercised strict control of the philosophical and theological content of books published in New Spain. Indigenous peoples were exempted from its surveillance, but the *Provisorato de Indios,* a special religious court, was responsible for judging Indian loyalty to the Catholic Church.[113]

A special court was set up for this purpose, and while the Inquisition was strict in its supervision of Spaniards and Criollos, it was allegedly less severe in its form as the court appointed over the Amerindians. While this eventually gave way to increasing severity, the belief that Indigenous "idols hid behind the altars" in New Spain was rampant—in other words, the fear of syncretism and clinging to Indigenous religious patterns was very real. This fear is the transatlantic version of the same fear of the *Conversos* and *Moriscos* in Spain, associated with the concern for *limpieza de sangre* and the worry over "crypto-Judaism" or vestiges of Muslim practice surviving a superficial conversion to Christianity.[114]

The Inquisition in Spain was highly suspicious of any lingering "Jewishness" or any Muslim garb or practices that might persist after conversion took place, and a division among Christians into "old" and "new" Christians was very real. "New" Christians—both *Conversos* and *Moriscos*—were watched with special vigilance. In New Spain, the recently converted Indigenous peoples were subjected to a similar scrutiny, and elements of Indigenous religious practice that persisted into their "new" Christianity were closely monitored. This is not to say that *all* such vestiges were stamped out, as the story of the Guadalupe event clearly indicates with its obvious transitioning of the goddess Tonantzin into La Virgen at Tepayec in 1531.[115] Notwithstanding this and similar instances of syncretism, the fact remains that many Indigenous records, poems, practices, stories, myths, and beliefs were virtually obliterated by the process of Christianization. Only the very first few years of missionary work in New Spain—carried out by Franciscans, Dominicans, and Jesuits before the First Provincial Council of Mexico in 1555—demonstrated anything even resembling a positive attitude toward Indigenous culture.[116]

What we now know as ethnographic research was carried out during this time, with the vast cache of drawings and notes compiled over the span of ten years by Bernardo de Sahagún (the *Florentine Codex*) being perhaps the best known. Similar work was done elsewhere, chronicling and drawing the Aztec and other tribes' myths, traditions, and lexicons. Although this was done with an eye toward improved proselytization, it still shows a sincere and positive approach to Indigenous culture and is worth bearing in mind as subsequent negative attitudes toward Mesoamerican culture develop. The initial stage of curiosity in the face of difference was short-lived: increasing Church bureaucratic presence and control after the First Mexican Council and subsequent councils curtailed the strategic leeway enjoyed by the first missionaries in Mexico/New Spain.[117]

With this in mind, then, Sor Juana's positive attitude toward the Mesoamerican rites portrayed in the *Loa* is exceptional, and would register as such in Spain. It is clear that Sor Juana cannot be said to inhabit the Mesoamerican world in her writing, oriented as she was toward the Baroque sensibilities of Spain. Nevertheless, her *tocotines*, preference for poetic ways of knowing and expressing truth (the *Sueño*), her *Loa* to *El divino narciso* demonstrate her curiosity (at least) and interest in Mesoamerican cultures. Significantly, too, her publisher's grooming of her image in Spain as a writer between Spanish and Mesoamerican cultures emblemizes her positive understanding of Indigenous religious elements in New Spain.

# Chapter 3

## The Challenge of a Cross-Cultural Religious Epistemology

| | |
|---|---|
| *Occidente poderoso,* | *Hear me, mighty Occident,* |
| *América bella y rica,* | *America, so beautiful,* |
| *Que vivís tan miserables* | *Your lives are led in misery* |
| *Entre las riquezas mismas:* | *Though your land is bountiful.* |
| *Dejad el culto profane* | *Abandon this unholy cult* |
| *A que el Demonio os incita.* | *Which the Devil doth incite.* |
| *¡Abrid los ojos! Seguid* | *Open your eyes. Accept my word* |
| *La verdadera Doctrina* | *And follow in the Path of Light,* |
| *Que mi amor os persuade.* | *Fully persuaded by my love.* |

—*Loa* to *El divino Narciso,* passage articulating the tension between the two religious expressions explored in the drama[118]

### Cultural Difference: Surface and Depth

In any situation of cultural encounter, the differences on the surface—food, music, language—constitute the most overt and malleable aspects of the encounter. Dietary differences are fairly easy (even fun) to share and explore among cultures, as are musical and linguistic differences. At deeper levels, though, perceiving and acknowledging differences becomes more challenging. In the fundamental category of *how we know what we know*—epistemology, in short—we find the deepest and least reckoned source of difference between cultures. How do various cultures constitute the process of knowing? Epistemological differences between cultures get even trickier when assumptions around religious knowing are being negotiated. How is religious experience categorized, articulated, communicated? Who gets to decide what is valid religious experience? Are the senses reliable in religious knowing, or is a mystical or aesthetic religious epistemology valued? Sor Juana's position as a religious writer between cultures brought her into questions such as these, though she may not have articulated them in these same ways. Nevertheless, we can explore how her work portrays and even melds the epistemological assumptions of both Mesoamerican and Spanish religious cultures.

## Sor Juana and Cross-Cultural Hermeneutics

Sor Juana's work exists between two cultures with two distinct sets of epistemological assumptions. The parts of her written work that utilize both of these or that attempt to harmonize these disparate approaches are among her most fascinating pieces. Her work in the *Loa* to *El divino narciso* personifies each and imagines aspects of an encounter between each way of knowing religious truth. From the point of view of present-day readers, and certainly from the point of view of her Spanish readership, her use of an epistemological mode in harmony with Mesoamerican ways of knowing constitutes a novel approach to the problem of religious experience and expression. Reason-based religious knowing can be limited by the very fact that it is a generally empirically-based approach to a subject (religious experience) that notoriously evades empirical analysis. How can religious experience be known by reason if it so often leads into "unreasonable" experiences—the ecstatic, the affective, the spiritual? When Sor Juana's works enter into conversation with Mesoamerican epistemological approaches, we find some of these challenges addressed.

Without disparaging the merits of a reason-based epistemology, watching Sor Juana engage the aesthetic epistemology characteristic of Mesoamerican religious culture identifies alternative ways that religious experience can be explored and conveyed to others.

## *Flor y canto* (flower and song): Mesoamerican Aesthetic Epistemology

*My flowers will not come to an end,*
*my songs will not come to an end,*
*I, the singer, raise them up;*
*they are scattered, they are bestowed.*[119]

*—Netzahualcoyotl (1402-1472)*

One of the challenges associated with investigating and communicating religious experience is that we are often frustrated by the culturally conditioned categories at our disposal for analysis and articulation of this experience. In a reason-based culture of religious experience, for example, we may feel compelled to translate subjective religious experience into various forms of provable propositions. Certainly when Sor Juana was writing, the Spanish theology and preaching she was familiar with were guided by the principles of reason. A fundamentally logical, systematic, and sequential model was assumed. As cultures met during the colonization of Mesoamerica, this logical approach to religious experience met the challenge of a profoundly different religious epistemology based on aesthetics, poetry, and mystical knowing. This is not to suggest that these elements were entirely absent from Spanish theology—they were definitely present. The privileged forms of assessing and communicating religious experience, though, were fundamentally *reasonable*. Likewise, it would be wrong to suggest that Mesoamerican religious thought was unfamiliar with something like an empirical approach to certain aspects of its practice. Nevertheless, the Mesoamerican approach differed substantially, and Sor Juana's work can help us appreciate not just how the two cultures differed but also how these two discrete epistemologies might hybridize and contribute to a more robust religious epistemology. Such an epistemology could be capable of capturing and expressing religious experience in new categories.

The epistemological mode of *flor y canto* or "flower and song" is a hallmark of Mesoamerican religious and philosophical systems extant at the time of Spanish colonization.[120] It was the product of centuries of religious practice and can be identified in various incarnations in virtually all of the varied tribal religious systems up to and including the Aztecs, whose pattern it was to assimilate the myths and iconography of those they conquered. At its fundamental level, *flor y canto* reflects the Mesoamerican understanding of truth (including religious knowledge) as multivalent, intuitive, heart-based, visual, and aesthetic. Poetic codification of *flor y canto* preserved fleeting glimpses of truth over time:

> ...for the ancient Mexicans, "flower and song," that is to say poetic expression, was the only way to authentic truth and, among all the comings and goings, even of civilizations, it was the only thing which was assured of a continued existence.[121]

Truth is multivalent inasmuch as it cannot be pinned down intellectually but is apprehended intuitively in an array of symbols and images. Truth is "heart-based," which reflects a Mesoamerican understanding of the physical location of the "organs" of knowing.[122] Truth is visual and fleeting—the "flower"—and is known through the experience of beauty in poetry, music, and "song."

*Flor y canto* as a privileged way of knowing in Mesoamerican culture developed alongside the religious understanding of balance in the universe. Mesoamerican creation myths typically involve some version of sacrifice, sometimes given willingly, sometimes achieved through trickery, but always made to ensure the continuation of creation. The forces of continuation and termination—life and death—were constantly in need of balancing, and sacrifice of the life force (either blood or actual lives) was the material necessary to maintain the balance.[123] Additionally, this balance was situated within a larger cycle of balancing or "tipping" from pole to pole, reflected in the cycle of the seasons and the reality of good years and bad years. These myths and cosmovision were developed in different ways by the Incas, Mayas, Olmecs, Toltecs, and others, and when the Aztec/Nahua tribes wandered from the northern reaches of Mesoamerican into the valley of what is now Mexico City, they incorporated Olmec and Toltec versions of the myths into their own systemization.[124] By the sixteenth century, when Cortés met the Aztec/Nahuas in Tenochtitlan, these disparate religious strains had been blended and assimilated by the Aztecs.[125] The understanding of sacrifice as a central factor in the maintenance of balance in the universe confronted the Spanish in the form of ritualized human sacrifice and blood-letting, and the Spanish misunderstanding of this practice led to widespread denigration and destruction of Mesoamerican religious systems.[126] It is important to note, however, that the notion of sacrifice in Mesoamerican religious systems had its basis in a particular cyclical understanding of the universe, and the importance of balancing this cycle was such that those sacrificed were almost certainly viewed as heroic or semi-heroic—and may in some cases have put themselves forward.[127] In cases where the captured enemies of warring tribes were sacrificed unwillingly, the symbolism and the understanding of balance still outweighed the apparent viciousness of the sacrifice; the internal logic of the universe demanded sacrifice for its continuation.

Maintaining cosmic balance was the basis for communal religious practice. This religious system generated the epistemological mode of *flor y canto* through the development of a priestly class who was able to discern the particular needs of the universe for achieving balance. Certain people could sense the appropriate measures to be taken to ensure the balance of the weather, the sun, the earth, and time. These seers developed into a class unto themselves, the *tlamatiname*: "those who know something."[128] The *tlamatiname* were poets whose vision gave them access to the mysteries of the universe. The poetic tradition that developed around the *tlamatiname* was marked by a preference for visual elements, symbolism taken from nature (each animal had its own personality and significance), and the understanding that the universe is fundamentally made up of a constellation of balanced dualisms.[129] The poetry composed by the *tlamatiname* explored these delicate balances and illustrated the way that they could be manipulated by human religious activity (including, but not only sacrifices). The poetry captured the myths of creation and related stories (and follies) of the gods. And the poetry that developed was created through the organ of truth perception, the heart—which was considered the seat of emotion and understanding.

Unlike the epistemological systems which were familiar to the Spaniards—based on empirical evidence, a basic trust in the ability of the senses to perceive reality, and the assumption that mind-based reason is the appropriate way to ascertain a monolithic truth—the *flor y canto* of Mesoamerica used intuition to generate *meanings* rather than *results.*[130] As a way of knowing, *flor y canto* used the aesthetic power of symbols, images, and music to discern the various truths and meanings in a given situation, reflecting the dualistic understanding of the universe and its fundamental multiplicity. The cult of the poet-king that developed in conjunction with this way of knowing was based on the sense that "those who know something" ought also to be those who gave order to the social structure—the rulers. Thus, one of the most famous Mesoamerican rulers, widely known even today, was both poet and king: Netzahualcoyotl (1402-1472), whose name means "the hungry coyote."[131] Epitomizing both the role of *tlamatiname* and ruler, Netzahualcoyotl was revered for his ability to penetrate the mysteries of the balanced forces of the universe, and his ability to articulate these mysteries was regarded as a way to manipulate them.[132] He saw the connection between beauty and truth, as well as the impermanence of human life:

> With flowers You write,
> O Giver of Life;
> With songs You give color,
> With songs you shade
> Those who must live on the earth.
>
> Later You will destroy eagles and ocelots;
> We live only in Your book of paintings,
> Here, on the earth.
>
> With black ink You will blot out
> All that was friendship,
> Brotherhood, nobility.
>
> You give shading
> To those who must live on earth.
> We live only in Your book of paintings,
> Here on earth.[133]

This passage clearly highlights the power of images ("paintings") and beauty ("flower" and "song"). Since it is written by a poet/king, we also get a sense of how these modes of apprehending divine truth were valued in this particular culture—poetry is neither decorative nor a leisure activity practiced by dilletantes. It is central to the religious and political life of the community, and its creation and promulgation helps maintain balance and a cosmic perspective within the society. And it is precisely here that we discover the power of this theopoetic way of knowing: if the balance in the universe and the preferences of the gods can be articulated (as in poetry and song), then it can be repeated, handled, known, and manipulated. The greatest fear would be to ignore a potential imbalance, so the poets who could articulate these concerns were massively important.

## *Flor y canto* and Sor Juana's Aesthetic Epistemology

The fact that Sor Juana was a gifted poet leads us to consider the ways that her work intersects with the poetic *flor y canto* epistemology of Mesoamerica. Two highly influential scholars of Sor Juana have reflected on her use of beauty as a way of knowing: George Tavard and Michelle González.[134] Tavard's work is earlier, and the subtitle of his work on Sor Juana indicates one of his central theses: "The first *Mexican* theology."[135] Tavard saw in Sor Juana the synthesis of the various cultural realities which she fused and incorporated into something novel, something uniquely "Mexican" rather than "New Spanish." His investigation explores the way that Sor Juana's work reflected the *theological* use of beauty as contrasted with its merely *decorative* use, an important distinction given the Baroque love of ornamentation. Likewise, Michelle González' *Sor Juana Inés de la Cruz: Beauty and Justice in the Americas* uses the theological aesthetics of Hans Urs von Balthazar, Alex García-Rivera, and Roberto Goizueta to explore the ways in which Sor Juana's work is shaped by the relationship between aesthetics and theology.[136] Both argue that Sor Juana is a *Mexican* writer because she incorporates elements of indigenous and Spanish culture into her work and worldview. *Flor y canto* is present implicitly, since a synthesized worldview naturally contains elements from each.

Clearly, something akin to the epistemological mode of *flor y canto* is present within Sor Juana's long poem *Primero Sueño* or "First Dream," to be explored more thoroughly later.[137] The fact that she uses poetic forms to explore the question of knowledge and knowing is in itself significant. Additionally, the poem narrates the soul's attempt to find a foundation from which to ascertain truth, and the journey is accompanied by many symbols and images of aesthetically pleasing objects from numerous cultural sources—birds from many environments, precious metals, precious stones, varying sources of light, and more. These images are significant in a poem investigating the basis for knowledge: they are not *decorative* but rather *indicative* of truth, suggesting its presence through their beauty, not unlike the way that the poetry of the *tlamatiname* used images to express divine truths. Ultimately, too, the *Sueño* ends without identifying a single, monolithic truth or a single way of seeing: meanings multiply, images pile up, and the soul–for all the beauty that it has seen—is not *assured* of truth. This is similar to *flor y canto* inasmuch as this Mesoamerican epistemology seeks more to *generate* meaning and multiple truths rather than to identify and "capture" a single, perceptible Truth.

*Flor y canto*'s location of truth in aesthetic categories entails a risk: in this system, the subjective nature of the perception of beauty means that truth can become fragmented—merely a matter of artistic taste.[138] The truths of the prophets, for example, was sometimes "ugly" or difficult to hear for its intended audience—far from beautiful, yet nonetheless true. Other instances of injustice where truth must be spoken to power raise the question of how far aesthetics can go in identifying truth. Who adjudicates the subjective perception of truth when power is inequitably distributed? Can those without the privilege of defining beauty in the public sphere—the disenfranchised, the poor, the physically or mentally ill—not see or speak truth? *Flor y canto,* then, is an attractive epistemological system on many levels, but it runs into the power dynamic inherent in all subjective definitions and perceptions of human experience: those with the power to enforce their opinions are those who adjudicate truth. If beauty and truth are linked and the definition of beauty is retained only by a privileged few, then potentially truth, too, is restricted. The social justice demand that truth be spoken into situations of injustice would need to be integrated into this way of knowing, and in fact Michelle González' work goes some distance toward making these connections. The power to establish the distinction between beauty and ugliness might be expected to be accompanied by other kinds of power and privilege, as in fact it was in the type of the "poet-king" revered by the Aztecs. The power to name beauty accompanied the power to order the population. Thus it is clear that there are many instances where beauty and truth are correlated, but also situations in which the truth as expressed by some might be experienced as "ugly" or threatening by others, or situations in which beauty as defined by the elite might prevent the expression of truth on the part of the disenfranchised.

Support for anything like a critique by Sor Juana of the mode of *flor y canto* is unrecoverable. She did not address it explicitly, and though her poetry makes use of the association between beauty and truth, the same could be said of many poets before or since. My sense is that her major critique of the ability to perceive and articulate truth through poetry (or any means) comes *in her act of silence* and her relinquishment of writing in 1693. After her run-in with Church authorities throughout the 1690-1692 sequence of the *Carta Atenagórica,* the response of "Sor Filotea," and her *Respuesta,* Sor Juana had perhaps written what she considered enough—and had her perceptions of truth suppressed and resisted. In this, perhaps she realized that the perception of truth (a charism of hers) could not survive the written expression of truth if no audience could be trusted to read it. What does it mean to see something true if the articulation of that truth creates resistance and oppression? This silence has been variously interpreted, but the interpretations I find most compelling always include an element of resistance and subversion rather than her own admission of guilt and acceptance of censure.[139] Seeing her silence as the ultimate repudiation of *expressing* truth—whether discerned through *flor y canto* or some other mode—gives Sor Juana agency in her silence and points a prophetic finger at the audience which was too limited to "read" her expressions.

## Working with Sor Juana Today

At this point it is helpful to repeat: cultural differences exist both on the surface of human experience (language, food, music) and at the base of experience (assumptions, ways of knowing, ethical commitments). The deeper values obviously influence the surface expression, as when music expresses the essence of a given culture. But these influences can be difficult to trace. Discerning base-layer cultural allegiances is difficult work precisely because these allegiances are seldom acknowledged even by those who are formed by a particular culture. Usually we become aware of such deep differences in assumptions when we come into contact with others whose assumptions differ from our own. In the moment of encounter, we realize that not everyone assumes the same basic things that we do about (for instance) how time is measured, how people know what they know, and how religious experience is constituted and shared. It often takes sustained encounter and conversation with others from other cultures before we are able to identify our own cultural assumptions. It is not an easy process.

In this challenging work, however, people like Sor Juana can be of extraordinary help. Sor Juana was confronted with a dizzying array of differences manifested between the cultures of Mesoamerica and Spain. There were superficial differences, of course, but at base, the differences between ways of knowing (epistemological differences) indicate the basic, perhaps often invisible differences that made the encounter so fraught. Even today, cultural differences at the root of our worldviews are the most difficult to reconcile: they are invisible and therefore challenging to address. For Sor Juana, the lens that most suited her looking into these differences was the lens of poetry. Her ability to navigate different epistemological modes is evident in her poetic work even more than in her more overtly theological writing. In her poetry, including the poetry found in her dramatic works, we discover some of the most fascinating insights of her work.

She is able to place disparate images from different cultures into conversation with each other. But the poetry that depends on these conversations between cultures is more than merely beautiful, and its effectiveness is more than merely the effectiveness of good poetry. Her poetry's use of disparate cultural artifacts actually helps us visualize more general conversations among or between cultures with different ways of knowing.

But how does this happen, and how can her poetry best speak to the challenge of interpreting (especially religious) experience in the face of cultural differences? In other words, how does her incredible gift for poetry move us closer to a cross-cultural epistemology? There is continuity between the theopoetic work of Netzahualcoyotl and the theopoetic work of Sor Juana. In neither case was poetry simply decorative. In both cases the poetic space they created was the space where theological insights could be generated through the interplay of disparate images. And especially in the case of Sor Juana, the poetic space she created was a culturally welcoming space: the images come from *both* of her worlds (Spain and Mexico/New Spain). The interaction of these images from her two worlds lifts the day-to-day experience of cultural encounter into a poetic space where the richness of this meeting can be explored and broad new theological insights can be appreciated.

## More than Decoration: Sor Juana's Theopoetics as Cross-Cultural Epistemology

For Sor Juana's poetry to be more than simply beautiful, it needs to aid the process of discerning truth within a poly-cultural context. The specific encounter between Mesoamerican and Iberian ways of knowing provides the context for these questions, but to see them most clearly, we need to add an additional voice to the conversation. We can be helped by thinkers who have entered into this (or similar) territory and who have added insights to the conversation. For our purposes now, we want to hear from a thinker who is familiar with both the history of the Mesoamerican/Iberian encounter in the $16^{th}$ century, as well as the ways that that encounter resonates into current-day conversations and religious ways of knowing.

One such thinker is Roberto S. Goizueta. Goizueta's work highlights the distinctive religious, cultural, and epistemological preferences of the Iberian and Mesoamerican peoples. Reading his work alongside the work of Sor Juana help elucidate the various dimensions of interculturality of her world. Goizueta and Sor Juana both reflect within an epistemological space giving credence to poetic, artistic, and intuitive insights, combining them with the propositional insights of theology done from a "scientific" perspective and pointing toward an approach to the divine which allows and encourages interdisciplinarity.

Even within a given culture, there are boundaries and borders present among various subcultures. Yet such distinctions seldom approach the vastly different realities which exist on parallel sides of two cultural entities which have deeply divergent linguistic, historical, and theoretical roots. A methodology rooted in theopoetics may be at least partially capable of speaking to the hermeneutical concerns of those standing at the boundaries, those who seek to (or are forced by circumstances to) navigate between and among cultures. Goizueta's influential article "U. S. Hispanic Popular Catholicism as Theopoetics" links epistemology with aesthetics, as he analyses specific examples of how Christianity is expressed culturally among Hispanics in the United States.[140] From the outset, Goizueta is clearly concerned with both the cultural expression of Christian forms and the way these expressions suggest an epistemological sufficiency in the category of the aesthetic. Beginning with a critique of "the devastating consequences of Western rationalism on Christian theology," Goizueta explores how "the theological enterprise"—for the purpose of his critique, at least, more or less coterminous with *academic* theology—has been stripped of the "traditional forms for communicating" knowledge of the divine.[141] The categories sidelined, he worries, have been "marginalized" and cast as suspect by the generally "rationalistic" elements in Christian theology as he sees it practiced. Given Sor Juana's preference (at least for the majority of her writerly career) for poetry, drama, and allegory, Goizueta's analysis of inclusion or exclusion of these elements in theological discourse is especially pertinent to a consideration of Sor Juana's contribution to theology and cultural studies.

After such a divorce between theology and the arts limned out at the beginning of his essay, Goizueta proceeds to suggest ways in which these traditional forms of theological knowledge might be returned to a contributive place in theological discourse. The forms he is especially interested in restoring include "symbol, ritual, narrative, metaphor, poetry, music, [and] the arts."[142] His entry point in for recovery of these categories is, as the title of his essay promises, "U. S. Hispanic Popular Catholicism." This culturally specific religious phenomenon, he contends, makes authoritative theological use of precisely the sorts of non-propositional categories of knowing that he hopes to restore to equal footing with a predominantly rational epistemology. Taking his cue from Amos Niven Wilder, Goizueta argues that the exploration of Christian revelation "requires" a methodology which includes categories as broad as the revelation itself: rationality alone is too limited a category for such a project. Goizueta employs Wilder's own language to emphasize this point: "We speak of a theopoetic because the theme of divinity requires a dynamic and dramatic speech."[143] Theopoetics here stands for a style of theological discourse that, while fully appreciative of the gifts rationality stands to offer, depends heavily on the communicative power of images and the affective power of any encounter with divinity. Emotional abstraction from the sphere of theological discourse may be a priority for some rational(istic) methodologies, but a theopoetic methodology invites affective contributions in an intentional and respectful way. Properly engaged, the emotions can contribute to theological clarity.

Further methodological clarification of the need for a theopoetic approach to the practice of Christian theology comes from Goizueta's reading of Hans Urs von Balthasar's *The Glory of the Lord: A Theological Aesthetics.* Goizueta chooses a memorable quotation to indicate his resonance with von Balthasar's analysis: "How could Christianity have become such a universal power if it had always been as sullen as today's humorless and anguished Protestantism, or as grumpy as the super-organized Catholicism about us?"[144] While the theological categories of "humorlessness" and "grumpiness" are amusingly flippant, one gets the strong sense that, with Goizueta, von Balthasar seeks a more deeply affective and playful theological methodology with an increased capacity for delight. Also present here is the sense that the affective, image-rich theological exploration *used* to exist—used to exist, that is, until "Western rationalism" rose to the ascendant methodological status it continues to occupy (though not unchallenged) today.

Proceeding carefully at this point, Goizueta pauses in his analysis of an overly rational theological methodology to preserve the balance between a reason-heavy form of theology and the theopoetic form that he has begun to propose: "To emphasize the theopoetic is not to suggest, however, that reason is an insignificant element of theological reflection or that aesthetic form is separable from theological content. On the contrary, *we must recover the fundamental unity* of what modern epistemologies and anthropologies have divided…"[145] Seeking to recover poetic and aesthetic forms of theological discourse does not mean that these forms can stand on their own as the only categories for such discourse. Goizueta's vision at this stage of his argument is holistic: in fact, according to his sense of the issue, the effort to recover aesthetic forms of theological knowing is virtually completely corrective.

It is at this point that Goizueta makes careful distinctions regarding precisely what he means by this "intersubjective" methodological proposal. Goizueta is aware of the potential pitfalls of a community focused only and inwardly on its "intersubjective action"—such a community's discourse could become hermetic, sealed outside of history, and thereby lose sight of the larger (historical and theological) community to which it might otherwise be accountable.[146] The danger of admitting affective categories into theological discourse (and perhaps why the link between such categories and strict rationality occurred in the first place) is that "'feelings' become ends in themselves, praxis becomes paralyzed."[147] If the emotions take over the ascendant position held by rationality, a sort of unhelpful (possibly solipsistic) chaos could ensue. One envisions a community immobilized by overly individualistic and sentimental interpretations of their own particular religious experience—an image of community that Goizueta is far from advocating. His hope is for balance, rather, a community nourished as each theological modality checks and urges the other to present its own unique contribution to the communal discourse.

Goizueta is right to be careful as he advocates for a more affective epistemological standard. The danger that comes with the presence of emotional epistemologies in theological discourse is analyzed by George Lindbeck in his 1984 book, *The Nature of Doctrine*.[148] Lindbeck sets out three models for the way that doctrinal statements can be understood to "operate" in construing community and ordering theological discourse. Among the models he proposes, what he calls the "Experiential-Expressivist" model sheds the most light on Goizueta's general project.[149] Lindbeck's category of the "experiential-expressivist" aspect of doctrine has similar positive contributions to the "theopoetic" model that Goizueta has begun to sketch. Like Goizueta, Lindbeck notes shortcomings in purely "discursive" (his adjective that more or less parallels Goizueta's "rationalistic") theology. Writing as if in direct conversation with Goizueta as he considers this model in contrast to a variety of others, Lindbeck clarifies his sense of the positive aspects of an "experiential-expressivist" understanding of theology:

> ...there is also room for the expressive aspects [in this model]. The aesthetic and nondiscursively symbolic dimensions of religion—for example, its poetry, music, art, and rituals—are not, as propositional cognitivism suggests, mere external decorations designed to make the hard core of explicitly statable beliefs and precepts more appealing to the masses. Rather, it is through these that the basic patterns of religion are interiorized, exhibited, and transmitted.[150]

With Goizueta, Lindbeck appreciates the powerful contributions that an aesthetic or theopoetic approach to divine revelation offers. Additionally, Lindbeck's caution regarding this contribution (at least as he imagines it operating in his "experiential-expressivist" model) echoes much of what Goizueta expresses. Theological discourse which takes subjective experience as its starting point becomes potentially chaotic when its "expressions" come into anything like conflict with the results of another's experience. In light of this risk, Goizueta is careful to retain a connection between theopoetic exploration in theology and a connection and respect for others in history who have engaged the same subjects: there is a constant need to test the results especially of an aesthetic methodology because its manner of "verifying" truth claims is relatively subjective. (Many post-modern analysts contend that "rationality" is no less subjective than an "aesthetic" or "affective" epistemology—there is no "balcony" on which one can stand to verify truth claims by a set of objective and immutable standards. Nonetheless, it may be that the established habits of rationality are such that truth claims can be verified within its well-established system in a way that a theopoetic approach does not currently enjoy.)

Sor Juana's gift for poetry is an ideal basis for the achievement of a cross-cultural epistemology. There are weaknesses both in the extremes of rationalism (dryness, stuffiness, coldness) as well as emotionalism (individual truths that have little connection with the community). The poetic vision she practiced throughout created space for both the rational and the emotional. Poetry by its very nature accepts images from many disciplines. Poetry is not limited to a particular source for its content: images from science, cooking, various religions, geographical surroundings, scriptures, and so on. Goizueta's voice is valuable because it highlights the risks of an overly rational approach, and Lindbeck helps us see the risks of an idiosyncratic emotional approach to theological truth. Sor Juana's theopoetics captures images from both symbolic worlds and holds them together in the same poetic creations. This is more than interdisciplinarity—it also allows images and contributions from different cultures to enter the same poetic space, each with equal honor and an equal right to be present. Theopoetic space is egalitarian space: images are brought together to serve the poem, and the interaction of these diverse images reflects an optimistic vision of how people from various cultural backgrounds might also find common ground for enriched conversation. Thus it is not naïve to wish for an epistemological approach to divine revelation that can function *in spite of* or *across* such cultural divides. Sor Juana's welcoming poetic vision, spanning the two worlds which surrounded and formed her, raises the hope that there is a space for cultural encounter that is harmonizing without obliterating the uniqueness or origin of the participating voices. Harmony in this case does not mean that some images are granted lesser or greater status based on their place of origin or relative status in the world. The theopoetic space allows these images from various cultures to interact.

The closing scenes of the *Loa* to *El divino Narciso* capture Sor Juana's magnanimous vision of cultures meeting in this theopoetic space. They have spent the entire *Loa* arguing and negotiating, living out real-world theological disagreements in the form of the poem/drama. Toward the end, the various voices begin finishing each other's sentences in a something like a statement of religious reconciliation: "America" and "Occident" (representations of the Indigenous religion) first show interest in the teaching of the Spaniards:

AMERICA

The magnitude of this you bring
As notices, as yet I cannot
Comprehend, of everything
I would know more, and in detail,
For I am moved by powers divine,
Inspired to know all you can tell.

OCCIDENT

An even greater thirst is mine,
I would know of the Life and Death
Of this great God found in the Bread.

Later, the Spaniards show a willingness to learn from the Native religious traditions, sensing that there is one divinity being represented via each of the distinct religious traditions:

Now are the Indies
All agreed,
There is but One
True God of Seeds![151]

And while the *Loa* is clearly somewhat playful in its representations of this conversation (and harmonizes the differences more readily than they were ever harmonized in the real world), the theopoetic vision represented here is generous and hopeful:

there is a poetic space in which this difficult epistemological conversation can be imagined, offering hope to those whose work it is to make sense of these differences in the in the world of actual cultural encounter. Visions of cultural encounter going well provide a necessary prologue to the encounters themselves, and it matters that Sor Juana uses poetry—not argumentation—to offer us these visions.

# Chapter 4

## Harmonizing Distinct Religious Epistemologies: Sor Juana's Theopoetics

| | |
|---|---|
| *Pues vamos. Que en una idea* | *That we shall do. I shall give you* |
| *metafórica, vestida* | *a metaphor, an idea clad* |
| *de retóricos colores,* | *in rhetoric of many colors* |
| *representable a tu vista,* | *and fully visible to view,* |
| *te la mostrare...* | *this I shall show you...* |

—*Loa* to *El Divino Narciso,* conversation between Western Religion and Indigenous American Religion

There are clearly places in cultural encounter where deep differences in religious ways of knowing come into tension. There is also an incredible *durability* in this tension: the encounter between Mesoamerican and Iberian ways of religious knowing continues into modern-day conversations around theology in the Americas. The fact that some of the reverberations set into motion 500 years ago continue to affect this conversation today show that finding a cross-cultural religious epistemology is difficult (and ongoing) work. But Goizueta's excellent article is also important for what it does not do: while it effectively illustrates the differences between Mesoamerican *flor y canto* ways of knowing and rationalistic ways of analyzing divine revelation, he does not move these differences toward harmonization. This may have been outside the scope of his article, and possibly an attempt to harmonize different religious ways of knowing is simply a conversation that needs more time, more discernment, and more contributions to become mature. In any case, Sor Juana's contribution here is essential, because she *does* appear to make an effort toward a cross-cultural religious epistemology in her work. To see how she does this, we can revisit the category of theopoetics to analyze popular religious practice in contrast to rationalistic theology—but now, we can expand theopoetics as a space for harmonization of the *two* rather than simply a characteristic of *one*.

We have seen that Goizueta names two clear epistemological options in his article, but his interest is more than taxonomic. He is also making a case that favors one over the other, at least in some regards. For example, Goizueta insists that "conceptual, logical reason is at home only in the rarified world of either/or and is stultified by the mestizo world of both/and."[152] In other words, the rationalistic way of knowing is confounded by the artistic, aesthetic, or image-based ways of knowing he has described. They are presented as incompatible, a sense which is more or less borne out by the fact that these tensions are centuries-old and still with us. Moreover, he states that in the face of the tensions between ways of knowing, reason-based thinking must "dissolve the tension into one of the polarities: either white or black, either European or Native American, either Latin American or 'American.'"[153] There is little hope for harmonization here.

But if Goizueta is less sanguine regarding the track record of European theology in light of these tensions, it is with good reason: for centuries, virtually the only participants permitted to engage in valid theological discourse were males trained in rationalistic ways of approaching the divine. Other voices were unauthoritative. In spite of his suspicion around these power dynamics, however, it is not enough to present theopoetic methodology as a solution to the overly rational theological system he attributes to rationalistic theologians—though it is definitely at least a partial cure. His example of the image-based religious knowledge represented by the Virgin of Guadalupe helps here. This image can be seen as the "ascendant" symbol of the eventual emergence of a cultural identity out of the encounter of worlds in sixteenth-century America, and it provides an alternative interpretation of the role of theopoetic images around cultural encounter. Where discursive language may be incapable of telling the complete story of the encounter, the image of Guadalupe captures the religious insights, affective elements, and poetic (though frequently tragic) nature of the meeting of these two worlds.

Especially as one living in colonized America, and as a theologian deeply concerned with poetic images, Sor Juana's relevance to a discussion of theopoetics and culture is clear. Somewhat in contrast with the model of theopoetic imagery set forth by Goizueta, though, Sor Juana seeks to discern poetic and theological images that *encompass* rather than *delineate* cultural differences. Her poetic vision reaches across the expanse of the globe to find images to include in the Soul's search for truth:

> Meanwhile, the blazing Father of Light,
> nearing the East,
> complies with predetermined codes and,
> with waning rays, signals farewell to
> distant antipodes:
> at some common point—from trembling light—
> creating their darkening Occident
> and our luminescent Orient.
> But first to pierce the darkness of the sky
> was Venus, the gentle,
> beauteous morning star,
> and with her Dawn, wife of Tithonus,
> —an Amazon robed in a thousand lights
> to vanquish night...[154]

This brief section finds Sor Juana's vision ranging through world mythologies, astrology, and a *positive* personification of the Americas (the "Amazon robed in a thousand lights"). This is cross-cultural (multicultural) theopoetics that accesses truth by using images from myriad cultures as stepping stones on its epistemological quest. Her efforts toward a theopoetic reading between and among cultures completes the image of theopoetics as a helpful methodology in cross-cultural religious dialogue. In the face of the substantial challenge of formulating a workable cross-cultural epistemology, Sor Juana's poetic work stands out as unusually successful and instructive for ongoing exploration.

## An Allegory of Epistemological Harmony: The *Loa* to *El divino narciso*

Sor Juana presents a playful yet compelling image of harmonization between cultures in her *Loa* to *El divino narciso*.[155] The *Loas* were brief dramatic pieces which were associated with longer *autos* or dramas.[156] In the *Loa* for *El Divino Narciso,* the cast of characters includes allegorical representations of various aspects of Mesoamerican and Iberian culture, notably "America, [Christian] Religion, Music, Soldiers, Musicians, Zeal, and Occident."[157] The language of the *Loa* itself demonstrates how this text encompasses representations of each of Sor Juana's two cultural locations. "Occident"—standing for Mesoamerican culture—is "a handsome Indian man, with a crown." "Occident" and "America…a gorgeously attired Indian woman" (who also stands as an exemplar of Indigenous culture) appear first in the drama and are addressed in the opening words by "Music":

> Noble Mexicans whose ancient line traces its origin to the sun's clear rays, since today is that happy day of the year when we consecrate the greatest relic of all, come adorn yourselves with tribal emblems so that devotion unites

> with joy to celebrate with festive pageantry, the great God of the Seeds.[158]

The *Loa* begins, therefore, with at least a verbal indication of high regard for the cultural and religious lineage of the Aztec festival; in the context of a Roman Catholic colony of Spain, this is in itself notable. Also significant in this passage is Sor Juana's broaching of theological (at any rate religious) issues at play in the cultural encounter between indigenous Mexican culture and Iberian Roman Catholicism. To open with a religious festival indicates that Sor Juana is prepared to explore the theological implications of encountering the culturally and religiously other through the vehicle of the drama.

The *Loa* continues along the strongly religious lines on which it opens, shifting toward the speeches of the two Mesoamerican characters (Occident and America) who interpret the meaning of their festival to honor the "God of the Seeds." As Music draws her introduction to a close, Occident relates the necessity of "human sacrifice": "two thousand gods are satisfied,/but human blood must be the price." Occident's language is pointedly reminiscent of the Christian trope whereby Christ's blood is seen as being shed for the salvation of all humankind—Sor Juana must know that the parallel blood symbolism will gain the attention of a Spanish audience while maintaining the content of the Mesoamerican rite. America seconds Occident's presentation of the general religious theme with her own enthusiastic paean to the "God of the Seeds," wondering rhetorically "What matters all the glittering gold/in which America abounds,/what value precious ores untold,/if their excrescences befoul/and sterilize a fertile earth,/if no fruits ripen, no maize grows,/and no tender buds spring forth?" Implicit (yet not entirely subtle) is a critique of the Spanish emphasis on the material wealth of Mesoamerica; it is in the voice of an indigenous figure that the ostensibly Spanish subject Sor Juana makes herself free to comment on Spanish mining practice.

Having thus dared to offer both a positive image of Mesoamerican religion and a critique of a key element of the Spanish colonial undertaking, Sor Juana has the indigenous characters exit. As America, Occident, and Music "exit dancing," the second scene introduces "Christian Religion" (dressed "as a Spanish lady") and "Zeal" (dressed "as a Captain General, armed") and a host of Spanish "Soldiers." Christian Religion opens the scene aghast at the tolerance of the preceding scene of abject paganism: "How is it, then, as you are Zeal,/your Christian wrath can tolerate/ that here with blind conformity/they bow before Idolatry,/and, superstitious, elevate/an Idol, with effrontery,/above our Christianity?" Zeal—a Spanish Captain, recall—calms Religion with a promise "their transgressions to avenge."

Up to this point, Sor Juana has portrayed the Mesoamerican religious festival using the same imagery of blood sacrifice known in Christianity and has painted a picture of Spanish Christianity as violent, vengeful, and jealous. The daring drama continues to unfold as America and Occident reenter the scene while Music plays. As the indigenous characters continue their dance in worship of the God of Seeds, Zeal and Religion argue amongst themselves as to the better approach: each wishes to convert the Mesoamerican idolaters to Christianity, but Religion "would go with tones of peace/(before unleashing your aggression)/to urge them to accept my word,/and in the faith be sanctified." Zeal, apparently temporarily stayed, adds haste to the proselytizing project by referring to "their revolting rite." Religion's opening gambit concludes on a noble note: "Open your eyes. Accept my word/and follow in the Path of Light,/fully persuaded by my love." America and Occident, disturbed that these newcomers are interrupting their worship, address Religion in an appreciative tone, asking "Oh, Lovely Beauty, who are you,/fair Pilgrim from another nation?" Religion introduces herself as "Christian Religion" and her discourse takes a prouder tack: "I propose that all will bend/before the power of my word." Within a few more similar exchanges—with the rhetorical temperature rising in stages—America and Occident decide to give up on the conversation and return to their festival and dancing.

Clearly upset at this rejection, Zeal ups the stakes with more impassioned accusations, demanding "How, barbaric Occident,/ and you, oh blind Idolatry,/can you presume to scorn my Wife,/ beloved Christianity?" Zeal continues in the face of Occident's reply with a further promise of vengeance and forceful conversion. "I am a Minister from God," Zeal proclaims, "Who, witnessing your tyranny,/the error of these many years/of lives lived in barbarity,/ has reached the limits of His grace/and sends His punishment through me." The swords of the Conquistadores, intimates Zeal, are "the instruments of Holy rage." Just as the confrontation reaches a fever pitch, Music chimes in with a chorus of "With festive pageantry,/worship the great God of Seeds!"

Unable to restrain himself further, Zeal summarizes his sense of the conversation thus far: "As our first offering of peace/you have so haughtily disdained/accept the second, that of war,/from war we will not be restrained!/War! War! To arms! To arms!" Significantly, it is the Iberians—whose violence was thematically present from the beginning of the exchange—who finally define the next step in this cultural encounter. Sor Juana unabashedly presents the Spanish evangelists as impatient, angry, and quick to interpret themselves as instruments of divine punishment for non-Christians. Her drama paints a picture of the Mesoamerican and Iberian cultural encounter as fraught with misunderstandings, hasty conclusions, and a too-quick reversion to physical violence and chauvinistic identification with the will of God.

Clearly overpowered but unconvinced of either their own wrongdoing or the rightness of Christian Religion and Zeal, America and Occident submit. In the moment of submission, however, Sor Juana gives Occident a powerful sentence that places him on the moral high ground: "Your declarations I defy/and only to your power yield." Once Zeal has conquered, Christian Religion stops the death-blow from the sword and offers another kind of "vanquishing"—"I shall win with soft persuasion." America quickly notices that the sword of Zeal and the words of Religion are deployed in an identical way, and she steels herself against the coming line of argument. The scene ends with Occident once again proclaiming his loyalty to the "great God of Seeds."

In the opening speeches of the next scene, the similarities between the blood sacrifice used by the Aztecs and the blood sacrifice at the center of Christian imagery begin to worry Christian Religion. "What reflection/do I see, what counterfeit,/thus patterned in their evil lies,/to mock our holy sacred Truths?" In the most overtly theological segment of the *Loa* thus far, America and Religion discuss the advantages of their respective religious systems; gradually, one begins to get the sense that the Mesoamerican religion espoused by America is making inroads into the religious imagination of Christian Religion. The similarities between the two—at first seen as evil mockeries perpetrated by the Devil—begin to emerge as points of mutuality and common value. As the conversation progresses, America, Occident, and Christian Religion discover that not only is their image of an embodied God that is internalized through ritualistic eating a common point, but they also share the practice of baptism. Occident immediately recognizes the need to be baptized as part of authentic religious practice: "Yes, this I know,/before aspiring to come near/the fruitful table, I must bathe;/that ancient rite is practiced here."

The distinction between Christian baptism and the cleansing rite practiced in Mesoamerica having been elucidated by Religion, the theological discourse continues toward some remarkable further points of commonality. Enthusiasm on both the American and Iberian side grows—and even violent Zeal begins to show signs of softening toward what he previously counted as a death-deserving idolatry. Eventually, a new idea dawns on Religion—she senses the advantage of using a "metaphor, an idea clad/in rhetoric of many colors/and fully visible to view,/this shall I show you, now I know..." Religion proposes to "show" the Mesoamericans the truth of the Christian faith, having intuited something about the epistemological preferences of the Aztec culture. Somewhat nervous about this new tactic, Zeal questions Religion as to the details of the proposed method. Religion explains: "An allegory it will be,/the better to instruct the two,/an *Auto* [longer sacramental drama] that will clearly show/America and Occident/all that they now beg to know." In a self-referential move which might well have been experienced as quite humorous— a common feature of Baroque sacramental drama—Sor Juana indicates that the play to be developed will be called *"Divine Narcissus,* for although/America, unhappy land, adored an Idol symbolized/by signs of such complexity/that through that Idol Satan tried/to feign the highest Mystery,/that of the Sacred Eucharist,/there was, as well, intelligence/among the Gentiles of this land..." The blood sacrifice and the rite of baptism demonstrate a readiness for the "true" nature of these practices—that is, the Christian nature.

Throughout the course of the *Loa*, the characters representing the various ethnicities, reified national identities, and allegorical emotional states ("zeal") discourse on the varieties of religious experience that each might claim as unique to its own position. Sor Juana enacts a simultaneously theological and poetic interpretation of the cultural encounter that surrounds her and is represented in her dual Mesoamerican and Iberian audiences. She attempts to transcend various cultural differences which otherwise might deepen into intractable divisions. Bringing drama and poetry into the conversation avoids the danger of a strictly propositional discourse which might fall flat; in the face of cross-cultural interpretation, categories and modes of verifying truth claims begin from widely divergent places. She is resisting an entirely reason-based way of knowing the divine. Sor Juana is convinced that the theological issues at stake in the cultural encounter between indigenous Mexican religion and Iberian Roman Catholicism should be explored in lush, image-rich dramatic poetry. The "propositional content" of the *Loa*, far from being hidden in this poetic form, is intimately linked to the aesthetic form employed. For Sor Juana, theopoetics offers the greatest opportunity to explore the scene of cultures meeting in Mesoamerica. It allows a dramatized, poetic, and suggestive negotiation of the religious systems that combine initially and eventually emerge from that encounter.

The characters representing the various ethnicities, reified national identities, and allegorical emotional states each speak on the varieties of religious experience that each might claim as unique to its own position. There are arguments and differences as well as coincidences and points of contact. It is a theopoetic conversation among participants from vastly different cultural locations. And as the drama comes to its surprisingly harmonious conclusion, the characters are able to join in a unified chorus:

> America, Occident, and Zeal sing: As we say, already the Indies know who is the true God of the Seeds! And with tender tears that pleasure distills, let us joyfully repeat with festive voice: (ALL) Blessed the day I came to know the great God of the Seeds![159]

This unification is a product of their theopoetic methodology, so to speak—they each contributed their voices and images to an open and poetic space, and religious knowledge that transcends each of their positions is the result. If Sor Juana is perhaps too optimistic about these disparate cultural and religious groups finding a joyful common ground, she nonetheless enacts a theopoetic reading of the cultural confrontation and encounter that surrounds her. Her efforts toward a synthesis—recognized by her own interpreters and symbolized emblematically in the frontispiece of *Fama y obras*—demonstrate the way that a theopoetic methodology might attempt to transcend at least some of the cultural differences which otherwise deepen divisions up and into our own time. Strictly propositional discourse falls flat in the face of cross-cultural interpretation because its categories and modes of verifying truth claims begin from widely divergent places. In a theopoetic cross-cultural epistemology, aesthetic categories—still problematic, but perhaps less linguistically conditioned—become the spheres in which the "truths" of cultural encounter can be to some extent negotiated. Combined with Goizueta's theopoetics which in some ways strengthen cultural identity (and, as a corollary, any boundaries drawn on cultural bases), the theopoetic methodology of Sor Juana Inés de la Cruz rounds out the repertoire of interpretive strategies in the face of cultural difference.

Theology is an elusive science: it seeks to approach the Divine with the clumsy tools of human knowledge and the natural limits of human language. At its best, theology approximates truth. Theology done at the intersection of cultures enjoys the added difficulty of negotiating a vast variety of linguistic, epistemological, and (often) power dynamics that must be taken into account as the discourse proceeds. A fundamental concern is, of course, an appreciation for culturally conditioned ways of knowing, seeking, and holding knowledge: some cultures proceed with a high degree of trust in an apparatus of formal, critical, and philosophical hermeneutic strategies. "Western rationalism" is the icon of this set of assumptions. In other cultures, such assumptions about the nature of theological discourse may not be as central, and any effort to enforce propositional categories in cross-cultural theological negotiation inevitably raises questions of problematic power dynamics—not to mention confusion and theological dead ends.

By proposing a theopoetics of religious experience and theological methodology, Goizueta seeks to fill in some of the gaps inherent in an overly-rationalistic approach to knowledge of the divine. In his reading, however, Goizueta risks overemphasizing the differences between Hispanic and Anglo culture, reversing the expectation that a non-propositional theological method might (to some degree) transcend rather than reinforce cultural boundaries. Theologians hoping to find common ground in cross-cultural theological discourse must augment Goizueta's theopoetic with something like the theopoetic of Sor Juana Inés de la Cruz: whether or not she was ultimately successful in navigating the often tragic confrontation of the Mesoamerican and Iberian cultural clash that surrounded her, she nevertheless attempted to take theopoetic images and place them in the service of cultural understanding and dialogue. The more that images such as the Virgin of Guadalupe become proprietary images associated with particular cultural identities, the more theologians seeking common ground for continued growth in mutuality find themselves alienated from one another.

## Theopoetics Between Cultures

Sor Juana's *Loa* for *El divino narciso*—particularly read through a theopoetic lens—brings us squarely into the territory of culture and epistemology. The question of how ways of knowing are shaped by cultural assumptions may be dauntingly broad, but specific aspects of it are inevitably raised in a careful reading of Sor Juana's work. Her long poem, *Primero Sueño (First Dream),* is among her most ambitious and overtly epistemological works. Sor Juana's *Sueño* reflects the epistemological encounter between Spanish and Mesoamerican cultures that formed its context and provides its subtext. A close reading of this poem clarifies the way in which Sor Juana's work gives space to various epistemological preferences. Her dearest epistemological source alongside the poetic is the *scientific.* Science as Sor Juana apprehended it is dissimilar from the concept of science as we know it now: it was (in the version she most admired) a collection of ideas, images, myths, guesses, and idiosyncratic/hermetic theories—a dizzying mix, and more poetic, really, than positivist. Vivid representations of the concept of science that surrounded her are seen in the work of Athanasius Kircher (1602-1680), a German Jesuit thinker whose approach to science was incredibly imaginative, creative, even surreal. Sor Juana's use of scientific tropes and images in her epistemological *Sueño* suggest a multivalent and multi-sourced way of knowing that resembles a *space* more than a *source*: knowledge is built in a poetic space that welcomes truths from various spheres of knowing. It is not sent to the mind only through an intellectual pipeline.

An epistemological preference of one culture may not be equally preferred (or indeed regarded at all) in another culture. One such preference which was at play during the seventeenth century encounter between Iberian and Mesoamerican cultures in New Spain was the (generally) Iberian or European preference for scientific ways of knowing.[160] Empirical observation, experimentation, and sequential testing of hypothesis were used to build knowledge. But could such scientific processes "build" religious knowledge? Many thinkers of the time believed they could. In the process of observing and portraying the cultural encounter between Iberians and Mesoamericans, Sor Juana recorded a number of striking epistemological insights. Sor Juana's use of a poetic epistemology (employing tropes and images from the world of science) works to include both the *flor y canto* aesthetic epistemology of Mesoamerica and the propositional/empirical epistemology of Spain.

How does terminology and the mode of casting questions create apparent methodological difficulties? Are there in fact distinct "types" of knowledge specific to various modes of inquiry and discourse? Do different cultures "know" in culturally specific ways, or is there a "universal code" which underlies superficial differences? If so, who has access to this code? These questions have been asked before. Sor Juana was among the many instances of similar quests to elucidate the relationship among methodologies and ways of knowing. Her vision provides Sor Juana with images and insights for her writing, especially her highly visual poetry. Others have investigated these aspects of her work, paying particular attention to her *Primero Sueño.* Among similar specific assessments of the *Primero Sueño*, literary and historical scholars read the poem as "a carefully constructed poetic composition designed to represent at its center an epistemological struggle to understand the whole of reality in rational terms."[161] This investigation concentrates more directly on the methodology *enacted* by the poem and the way in which Sor Juana creates an epistemologically welcoming space in her poem.

## The *Sueño*

The *Primero Sueño* or *First Dream* was Sor Juana's most ambitious poem.[162] The *Sueño* is a poem of 975 lines. Sor Juana probably composed the poem sometime between 1688 and 1692.[163] The poem is a *silva,* an established Spanish poetic form "which uses the basic Spanish classical lines (either eleven or seven syllables long, corresponding to the iambic pentameter in English) irregularly combined and rhymed in an order that does not repeat itself in stanza form."[164]

According to Sor Juana's own assessment, the *Sueño* is also her most personal poem: "I have never written anything of my own free will, but rather because of entreaties and commands of others, so that I cannot recall having written anything for my own pleasure except a little scrap of a thing they call *El Sueño.*"[165] Disingenuous though this reference may be, it suggests that the *Sueño* contains her most decisive—in any case, personal—treatment of the questions and struggles that kept turning up in her studies and compositions. In contrast with her commissioned works and popular and sacramental dramas, the audience for the *Sueño* appears to have been first Sor Juana herself—and then interested others.

The poem has been subjected to multiple attempts to schematize its 975 lines—some are quite elaborate. George Tavard in his *Juana Inés de la Cruz and the Theology of Beauty: The First Mexican Theology* harmonizes multiple organizational schemas for the poem and arrives at a six-part division:

| Line #'s | Theme |
|---|---|
| 1-80 | the coming of night |
| 81-233 | night, the sleep of the universe |
| 234-291 | the origin of dreams |
| 291-780 | description of one special dream |
| 781-886 | the awakening |
| 887-975 | the return of day [166] |

The individual narrator of the poem is a trope of Sor Juana's autobiographical self; more analytically, scholars like Elias L. Rivers discern "an active intellect that soars and struggles to understand the whole world in a self-conscious, rational way."[167] According to Rivers, this "protagonist" and her aspirations illustrate Sor Juana's "peculiarly modern scientific curiosity."[168] The poem reaches into the natural world unapologetically in its pursuit of the necessary material for its epistemological discernment. Within the "scientific" purview, moreover, is Sor Juana's sense that images from scientific observation of the natural world contain, mirror, or refer to truths about a world of divine order and power. The natural world is constantly speaking not only its own order, but also a more or less "secret" order that is available to those prepared to discern it.

Sor Juana and her Baroque contemporaries wanted to believe in some sense of the knowableness of the divine world through and within the natural world—thus their interest in science. But the process of gaining access to the divine codes of the universe was never straightforward. In the *Sueño*, Sor Juana expresses doubts and hopes around the intellect's ability to perceive and to know divine truth through sensing the natural world. It becomes clear that these attempts sometimes end in frustration or further questions rather than conclusions. Octavio Paz' influential reading of the *Sueño* makes clear that the poem does not merely eulogize a knowledge that that is desired but impossible to grasp: "*First Dream* is not a poem about knowledge as a vain dream, but a poem about the act of knowing. This act adopts the form of a dream...in the sense of a spiritual voyage."[169] If with Paz, we take the *voyage* as the controlling metaphor, the destination remains unclear—and is perhaps a secondary concern.

The poem opens with an image of the earth casting pyramid-shaped shadows upward "toward the Heavens."[170] The shadows—"obelisks"—"attempt" to reach the stars, but cannot reach; silence reigns. The image that follows is of a screech owl—the mythical Nyctimene—wriggling its way into a temple and drinking the oil out of the "holy lamps where burn eternal flames"—and the lamps go out. Gradually, and attended by similarly Baroque images, the narrator of the dream enters a phase of deep sleep. Any *Sueño* begins, of course, in sleep. As is often the case, however, it takes time to *fall* asleep—in this poem, there is a sequence that simulates this "falling." The first image we encounter in the poem is the image of night: the "Pyramidal, doleful, mournful shadow/born of earth." In this instance, the darkness is related to an "attempt...to ascend." This theme of thwarted ascent (toward knowledge) is not fully developed until later in the poem, but it is notable that it appears at the outset (4). The darkness is given weight by "mist" and "exhalation" (17, 18). It hovers over "a silent kingdom" in which "only muted voices could be heard" (20, 21). The opening picture, then, is utterly sensuous, and not a little ominous: the darkness is constituted not only by an absence of light, but is intensified by humidity, as well as an aural heaviness which "mutes" and "muffles" (24) any sounds or voices.

Having set the poem into motion—or into stillness, rather—with these images of darkness and silence, Sor Juana begins to populate the (thus far) straightforwardly sketched scene with characters from a variety of legendary sources. A "humiliated" bird appears in the heavy darkness—Nyctimene, the erstwhile daughter of Epopeus turned into an owl by the goddess Minerva,—and is seen "lurk[ing]...at the chinks in sacred doors" (28). The sense is of a temple, though the building in which the owl "lurks" is not named or described in detail.

The owl begins alone, drinking the oil from the various lamps in the temple. Soon Nyctimene is joined by goddesses Diana and Minerva, and the trio commence a song—"a tuneless and appalling *a cappella*"—which is more "silences than sound" (57, 59). The strains of this "gloomy" music bring sleep, but by such a circuitous path that the poet uses lines 70 through 147 to describe its onset: "Sleep, in summary, now possessed all things, all things were now by silence overtaken" (170). Chronologically, the poem is now at "the darkest hour of the night,/shadow marking midpoint to the dawn": it is midnight (151-152).

Sleep is compared to the image of death; particular attention is paid to the way in which death comes to those from high and low estate alike, with the poles represented by (among others) the Pope and a "lowly rustic in his hut of thatch" (183, 185). With these preliminaries satisfied, Sor Juana gives the "soul"—the central character of the poem from here on through—freedom to explore the dream. This freedom is imagined as freedom from "governing the senses," or a sort of freedom from administrative duties (193, 197). The senses are "dead" in sleep, leaving the soul free of the responsibility of gathering and ordering input.

Various bodily organs receive attention and address before the soul's journey is described. The heart, lungs, the tongue (silent, now), and the stomach, among others, are each considered in relation to the orderly functioning of the body. For Sor Juana, the heart is the "core of vital spirits," while the lungs are "magnet[s]" that attract cool air and release it slightly warmer—the air "steals" a bit of bodily heat with each breath (210-225). This sequence is remarkable for its ability to illustrate the quality of the freedom which the soul is beginning to enjoy (and which will allow its upcoming journey)—the soul's responsibilities, imaged through the organs' functions, are myriad. A subtle undertone of neglect of responsibility, though, is impossible to ignore, and is perhaps vaguely autobiographical—her literary work eventually came into tension with her identity as a nun.

Throughout the description of these organs—preparatory to the soul's release—Sor Juana continually invokes silence. The tongue is silent, and it is a silence of constraint—*enmudecía,/ con no poder hablar*—there is no "power" for speech, to read the double entendre of *poder*. Likewise, the body's "warmth" is the "silent indication" that life persists—otherwise, the sleeping figure is *un cadáver con alma*—a cadaver with a soul (200-205). Physical life is intimately close to physical death, and the soul's freedom from integrating the work of the senses and the organs is a step yet closer to complete death. Significantly, then, as this portion of the poem develops, an image of life and death emerges which suggests a spectrum rather than a binary opposition. Wakefulness is at one pole of this spectrum, and complete death at the other. Between these exist sleep (an image of death, but attended by the soul) and dreaming sleep (an image of death, again, but with the soul demonstrating a sort of "independence" and agency). In light of Sor Juana's two "deaths," such an image provides a category for interpretation that might be lost if a purely "either/ or" notion of "death/life" were applied to the end of her work and the end of her physical life. And though perhaps unavailable to Sor Juana in the confusion of her first (literary) death, readers seeking images to explore the vacuum of her final years can find a point of orientation in such a spectrum.

By line 223, the images begin to shift from mythological themes to natural themes; scientific images are referenced for the first time overtly in lines 234 and following in a long description of the working of the human body and its relationship to the mind: "That most competent and scientific laboratory,/dispensing warmth to all the body,/withholding never, ever diligent,/neither to the neighbor showing preference/nor slighting one remote,/

with nature's instrument is taking note/of precise measurements/ of [partially digested food] it will assign throughout the soma,/ distilled by unremitting heat, and then,/in selfless sacrifice (benevolent/its intercession) between Humidity/and fire impose itself, and, paying the price,/give up its substance..." Energy migrates from the "furnace" of the body to "stoke" the mind. The conglomeration of striking images of the human body as furnace, machine, and instrument display Sor Juana's comfortableness and creativity in the face of scientific images, and she introduces them into her poetic composition just as epistemological questions begin to take center stage.

Eventually, the images of the body unwind and transition into images of and for the mind (lines 250 and following). Sor Juana assigns the "human heat" generated by the "cauldron" to become "mist" which wafts to the mind and produces (in hierarchical sequence) "reason," "imagination," "memory," and "fantasy." From this sequence of images comes a sense of the "origin" of dreams. Interestingly, by rooting the origin of dreams (including the dream about to be narrated in greater detail) in the physical body—rather than in a metaphysical force outside the body—Sor Juana prefers a physical and material "location" for the revelation to follow; the scientific images of the body lead back and forth between images of revealed knowledge and insight. The conversation space is open to images from each epistemic realm. First mythology, then science, combine to create her investigation into what is finally knowable.

The place in which the images—whether of the body or the metaphysical realm—are synthesized is introduced in line 292 as "the Soul." The Soul is able to collect images and insights from within the dream and hold them in creative tension with each other. Once the images from various sources are collected within the purview of the Soul, the Soul's work becomes evident: how do the images work together to create, generate, or indicate knowledge? It is at this point that Sor Juana's poem begins to introduce the notion that anything like conclusive knowledge may need to be indefinitely postponed: the ascending intellect struggles to organize and interpret the "material" presented in the dream. Paz is helpful in elucidating the sense of challenge the Soul confronts in the face of the material: "The endeavor 'to investigate nature' is revealed as a task whose weight would crush a Hercules, or Atlas himself."[171]

Now that the soul finds itself "transmuted into/beauteous essence and discarnate being," its journey—so far much anticipated, but as yet not embarked upon—begins. The poet takes a final lyrical moment to hover over the soul's freedom within the dream:

> ...free of all
> that binds her, keeps her from liberty,
> the corporeal chains
> that vulgarly restrain and clumsily
> impede the soaring intellect that now,
> unchecked, measures the vastness of the Sphere...
> (297-302)

This freedom, however, immediately comes up against images of freedoms thwarted or rebuffed: alongside the massive twin pyramids that the soul begins to apprehend, we find images of "the mighty Titan, Atlas, [who] an elf became," as well as "Mount Olympus,...humbled..." (310, 314-315). If other mythical ascents are any indication, this ascent will likewise be filled with risk.

For the course of the description of the two pyramids, Sor Juana continually returns to notions of the punishment that comes to those who overreach: simply gazing upon these pyramids has consequences. The "questing eye,/exhausted now, and overcome with awe" has made its way up the pyramids and finds itself completely overcome by the sight. In fact, the gaze down the pyramids makes the eye "dizzy," and a sensation of pain ("punishment" in Peden's translation) ensues—and all because the eye "ventured to give vision wings" (354-368). The twin pyramids—"artificial Mountains"—are subsequently joined by the image of the Tower of Babel and "dolorous signs of which today/(not ruins, but asymmetries of language/that a voracious time does not erase)" (412-417). The heights of the pyramids recall the height of Babel as well as the consequences of the aspirations which built it; the location of the punishment in language is particularly significant in the context of a verbal composition such as the *Sueño*. Thus the soul, free from the constraints of the body, reckons itself constrained by the pattern of ascent-and-punishment that it apprehends. The soul marvels at what it is able to see, but begins to feel fear:

> [The soul] cast her gaze across all creation;
> this vast aggregate,
> this enigmatic whole,
> although to sight seeming to signal
> possibility, denied
> such clarity to comprehension,
> which (bewildered by such rich profusion,
> its power vanquished by such majesty)
> with cowardice, withdrew. (445-453)

A "repentant vision" abandons its initial ambitions, deciding not to look into the sun, nor to aspire to the great heights that continue to attract and frighten the soul simultaneously. Adding further images of the negative consequences to her poem, Sor Juana invokes the image of the sun burning anything which comes to close to its heat, and recalls Icarus and his well-known plummet from his own ascent.

The poem proceeds to follow the soul in its dream of complete knowing. A variety of insights come, vast numbers of images are processed, but the soul remains frequently confounded by "awe" and "wonder," as if the matters gazed upon do more to baffle it and overcome its faculties than they do to educate it. Gradually, the soul begins to question its aspirations, and in a series of powerful moments toward the end of the poem, the poet invokes images of daring and ambition ending in tragedy—the image of the glory-seeking sailor "rashly seek[ing] his doom/in order to immortalize his name" ends in an image of punishment again (800 & ff.). Again, silence operates in the post-ascent image: we find the wish that "the punishment were never known,/that the offense not be repeated;/rather, that prudent silence—judicious/statesman—muffle tidings of the consequence" (800-815). In an amazing parallel with Sor Juana's own eventual punishment and silence, her poem here links the two, suggesting that the consequences of intellectual daring and risk-taking end with tragedy that must not be made known. The silence, though, is not itself the punishment, but a strategy to avoid encouraging others to act in similarly ambitious ways. The poem says it best:

> [N]ews of a compelling action is
> its greatest danger,
> as contagion spreads with every telling:
> far better that the deed remain unsung
> and not taught as admonition;
> less heeded, less the chance of repetition. (821-826)

Autobiographical notes in the *Sueño* are difficult to overlook. Especially read in the knowledge that Sor Juana herself would be "punished" for daring to "give vision wings," this poem—full of images of intellectual freedom and daring, yet fraught with the promise of its consequences—provides a hermeneutical key for reading Sor Juana's first death.

The *Sueño* investigates and catalogues a variety of sources of knowledge, each in turn asked to contribute to the overall search for divine truth. A remarkable synthesis results. And while the poem does not conclude with a sure knowledge, it does not despair, either: the poem itself stands as an emblem of the search for knowledge and suggests the multi-faceted nature of knowledge. Images and insights from a variety of sources interact and surround the narrator with something perhaps superior to final, conclusive knowing: a sense of the spiritual goal associated with the search, and a sense of the gifts each methodological schema can contribute to this search. It is, finally, a beautiful and hopeful image of interdisciplinary epistemology that results.

A poetic epistemological framework for cross-cultural religious conversation would welcome insights from various disciplines. The primary *contribution* of such a framework would be a shift in the metaphors used to describe the interaction: from conversation space to poetic gathering place—from which a number of implications could follow. The primary *difference* would be a shift from the sense of each discipline contributing *propositional truth* to an image of each discipline contributing *images*. Propositional truth is not abandoned—it is simply imagined differently.

In a poetic framework, issues of the epistemological validity or verifiability of each or either contributing discipline would be secondary—not because such validity is unavailable or unimportant, but because the question of primary importance relates to the ways in which the images interact, virtually regardless of the systems which may have generated them. Sor Juana's poetic *bricolage* assembles images from a wide variety of sources, disciplines, fables, myths, and so on. That some of these elements have since been discredited—such as, for example, her obsession with Egyptian hermeticism as the "system of systems" uniting all historical insight—does not in the least diminish the poem's ability to move the reader toward greater clarity on its chosen subject of epistemological relationships.

Some might posit a radical discontinuity between what Sor Juana understood as science in the seventeenth-century Baroque period and what is typically meant by the same term today. Nonetheless, in spite of innumerable developments and paradigm shifts, the idea that scientific inquiry is in some essential way "beyond" its earlier manifestations depends too heavily on myths of progress and infinite refinement. Progress has indeed been made, as medical science alone is sufficient to prove. On the other hand, the cycle of hypothesis, experiment, observation, and conclusion was as familiar to Sor Juana as it is to the current scientific community. We might do well to consider ways in which a pattern of continuity rather than discontinuity best describes the trajectory of scientific development over the intervening three hundred years. Paz is clear on this point, too: "It must again be emphasized that without hermeticism, alchemy, and magic speculations, the empiricism of modern science would not have been possible."[172]

A poetic epistemology gathers images from eclectic—even divergent sources—and allows them to interact while the poet simultaneously suspends any assessment of their truth content. This is not to suggest that truth content is not an important category. It is to suggest, however, that the knowledge generated depends as much on the interaction of the images contained in the poem as it might on the relative veracity of any individual component. A poetic epistemology assumes that gathered images, tropes, and insights from eclectic sources find some harmony—if only as a function of the "singleness" of the individual authorial self "holding the pen." The fact of a single poet or even a single poem allows multiple elements in proximity and juxtaposition to interact, jostle, and create meaning and knowledge unavailable to any of the systems operating on their own.

The metaphor of a poetic and welcoming space suggests an image of for the larger conversation between cultures that emphasizes an egalitarian approach to images and insights generated by various methodological systems. This approach—a theopoetic approach, gathering visual elements to create a synergistic complex of images—can be coupled with a willingness to suspend (if temporarily) an evaluation of any given image from any given discipline against the methodological standards of another. A picture of disciplines as contributive to a central quest is emphasized, leaving open the possibility of an interaction among methodologies which avoids a preference for scientific positivism on the one hand and wild metaphysical speculation on the other.

A comprehensive system for evaluating the outcome of this interaction of images and insights is impossible to construct. Allowing a poetic space for the conversation among methodological insights resists the urge to arrive at anything like a synthesis. The combination of images in Sor Juana's poetry does not fix the anxiety which may attend a multi-disciplinary approach, but allows the interplay among the images simply to exist and persist. This is not to say that something like a synthesis or end point cannot be hoped for, only that the category of "outcome" is bracketed in favor of a category of eclectic "income" of images. A poetic space for the conversation permits the jumble of images to be taken as a provisional and acceptable result.

As Sor Juana the poet is able to place elements of discrete systems within the same poetic universe, so too are those concerned with the interface cultures able to move current insights from each into proximity with each other and observe the ways in which they interact. For Sor Juana, this depends on an underlying urge toward harmonization of various epistemological methods; stated distinctions among science, philosophy, literature, and mythology work as short-hand rather than categorical assignments unable to be broached. To place an epistemological framework within the category of poetry is not to enact a relativist suspicion that nothing can be known: placing insights alongside each other without immediately evaluating their truth content postpones but does not abjure the need to ascertain accuracy, validity, or authenticity.

Additionally, far from being merely a Baroque attempt to place disparate images in juxtaposition with each other and to watch the sparks fly, Sor Juana's ability to gather and welcome knowledge from a variety of epistemological systems—some empirical, some overtly mystical—is an instance of its own epistemological convictions. Knowledge is—to use a more recent phrase—inherently interdisciplinary. Above this, though, and especially for those whose religious faith is part of their epistemological investigation, Sor Juana demonstrates a method by which the divine truths usually assigned to the category of "revelation" can emerge from the data gained by empirical observation. As Paz notes, "Sor Juana defends her love of the secular sciences as being a path toward the divine: this attitude was more philosophical than Christian, as her critics and censors did not fail to point out."[173] Whatever ratio of "philosophical" to "Christian" knowledge Sor Juana prefers, she in any event is comfortable combining both.

Sor Juana's *Sueño* represents a model for further understanding the nature, promise, and methodology of current instances of epistemological "sorting"—especially as broached by the encounter of persons from various cultural backgrounds and preferred ways of knowing. This theopoetic methodology resists anything like a final assessment of the propositional truth content of the "invited" insights and images, and instead delights in their generative and creative mix. The postponement of propositional assessment is transformative: poetic energy derives from the interaction of the images and is not defeated by any image's relative veracity. With this emphasis in place, the nature of epistemology as pilgrimage emerges. Pilgrims from various disciplines participate in an ongoing effort to take the images of their own methodologies and welcome them into a gathering space where their interaction and synergy lead toward knowing.

# Chapter 5

# Speaking Knowledge: Dynamics of Participation in Communal Discourse

*Rhetoric—unless subordinated to dialectic or perhaps the ironies of its own art—is a dangerous commodity, indifferent to truth and morality.*

–David Jasper[174]

## Into the Public Sphere: Sor Juana's Entry into Public Theological Discourse

For Sor Juana, the tension between *knowing* and *speaking* was lived out in a dramatic chain of events centered around a series of publications and letters. While her desire for knowledge was an intensely personal and even private experience, negotiating access to the wider conversation about this knowledge became gruelingly public. An exchange of letters between Sor Juana and the masked and re-gendered persona of the Bishop of Puebla, Don Manuel Fernández de Santa Cruz y Sahagún, began after Sor Juana responded in writing (at the Bishop's invitation) to a sermon composed by Portuguese Jesuit Antonio Vieira.[175] Although the exact date of the sermon's composition is difficult to ascertain, it is generally held that it was composed between 1640 and 1652 and read by Sor Juana in a Spanish translation published in 1677.[176]

The content of Vieira's sermon included a variety of novel Christological constructs and proposed strong readings that contrasted with three of the doctors of the Church: Augustine of Hippo (354-430), Thomas Aquinas (1225-1274), and John Chrysostom (c. 347-407).[177] Upon Bishop Fernández' prompting, Sor Juana wrote a theological response especially concerned with the Christological insights explored in the sermon, apparently unaware that her critique would be published.[178] Bishop Fernández received Sor Juana's observations and christened the critique *Carta Atenagórica* or "letter worthy of Athena." His intentions at this point are far from clear, as he had been sympathetic to Sor Juana's work previously and was probably not engaging in entrapment. Later, though, after the *Carta Atenagórica* had garnered much attention, Bishop Fernández continued the exchange with his *Carta de Sor Filotea*—"Letter from Sister Philothea," writing behind the mask of a concerned fellow nun encouraging Sor Juana to leave theological thinking well enough alone.

When Sor Juana replies with her written "Answer," the famous *Respuesta a Sor Filotea*, we gain access to Sor Juana's thinking around the rights of women to participate in theological discourse. What's more, her *Respuesta* sets into motion the chain of events that eventually leads to the cessation of her public writing—her silence—and raises a host of questions about the nature of access to public religious discourse. Throughout the exchange of letters, the writing on both sides is marked by rhetorical masking (of either identity or intent), double meanings, and veiled threats. More than in most of Sor Juana's poetic work, then, attending to the rhetorical strategies deployed throughout the exchange of letters clarifies what is most fundamentally at stake: the power to participate in theological discourse. Above all, the exchange demonstrates the way that subtle rhetorical and linguistic strategies were used (and can be used still) to mask power, limit access to public discourse, and control individual voices. On the other hand, Sor Juana's expert use of these same tactics in her *Respuesta* powerfully shows how such circumscription can be subverted and resisted. Thus the nuances of the language used (and the silences between words) form an essential part of understanding how Sor Juana's cross-cultural and religious epistemological insights attempted to gain her entry into the larger conversation of public theology.

As noted above, the first publication in the exchange is known as the *Carta Atenagórica* (November of 1690)—written by Sor Juana, but then published by Bishop Fernández without her prior consent. The follow-up piece, *Carta de Sor Filotea*, is Bishop Fernández writing as a fellow nun.** The third piece of the exchange, and among Sor Juana's most famous and influential works, is the 1691 *Respuesta a Sor Filotea*, in which she argues (among other things) for the rights of women to participate in theological education and discussion. Bishop Fernández' *Carta de Sor Filotea* represents the first rhetorical "move" in the exchange. The Bishop uses a female persona, and with this step we see how language has already begun to operate in an indirectly persuasive way: his power is masked, and his admonishments are presented as sisterly care and concern. Whether advice in the *Carta de Sor Filotea* is sincere or not has been debated in the critical literature on the subject—some have proposed that the Bishop's initial publication of the *Carta Atenagórica* was intended to give Sor Juana an opportunity to defend herself and demonstrate her worthiness in and for theological discourse.[179] Most readers, however, follow Sor Juana's own interpretive bent in this matter, summarized in the *Respuesta a Sor Filotea:* "...not even the permission for publication has been a decision of my own, but the decision of others beyond my control."[180] Moreover, the *Carta de Sor Filotea* in response to the *Carta Atenagórica* urges Sor Juana to change the focus of her study: when s/he asks Juana to "improve [her study] by sometimes reading the book of Jesus Christ", we discover indications of the prescriptive power wielded behind the persona

* Later publications of this exchange append the Bishop's letter directly to Sor Juana's critique of the sermon, though it is likely that some time passed between the publication of Sor Juana's thoughts and the Bishop's eventual *Carta de Sor Filotea*.

of the bishop.[181] The exchange, it seems, is not framed in order to exonerate Sor Juana but rather to frame a larger debate around the nature of the community and the appropriate use of Juana's (and women's) theological power and intellect.

Indicative of the sensitive communal concerns being indirectly negotiated beneath the surface of this exchange, an ironic tone in the *Respuesta* comes across at times quite intensely. Irony is especially close to the surface when Sor Juana gives a masked account of the way in which her written critique of Vieira's sermon came to be appropriated and published without her consent:

> ...when the letter that you saw fit to name Athenagoric, was delivered into my hands I burst into tears—a thing I do not do easily—of confusion at your kindness, which appeared nothing less than a reproach from God to the wretched way I respond to him.[182]

A language palette which includes "confusion" and "reproach" is decisively tinted toward irony when used in this ostensibly grateful passage. Sor Juana's tears are, we suspect, less than joyful. We are left with a distinctively ironic sense for the remainder of her *Respuesta*, not least because she addresses the "mask" of the Bishop of Puebla rather than addressing his identity overtly. It is generally accepted that the true identity of the Bishop writing as "Sor Filotea" was known; nevertheless, by sustaining the assumed identities throughout her *Respuesta*, Sor Juana manages her own sort of masking process. At the discursive level, her *Respuesta* operates "merely" as a letter from one nun to another, peer to peer, woman to woman. At the level of implication and connotation, however, the secret is out: the flow of hierarchal and theological authority beneath the surface is where the truly powerful current exists.

Sor Juana is keenly aware, too, of the presence of masked power in "Sor Filotea's" introductory *Carta de Sor Filotea* joined to her *Carta Atenagórica*. She hints at the presence of this power with daring openness: "Though it was clothed as advice, it will have for me the substance of a command."[183] In a very real way, the letter of "Sor Filotea" does equal a command, and Juana's temerity in her *Respuesta* is only highlighted by her playfulness in the face of "Sor Filotea's" enforceable suggestions. Sor Juana's clever choice of words here maintains for her a sort of agency as she "chooses" this particular interpretation of "Sor Filotea's" suggestions—in an exchange such as this, the *choice* to maintain the illusion of masked identity is significant.

## That Which is Said and Written: *Lo Decible*—"The Sayable"

In the "Prologue" to his incomparable biography and interpretation of Sor Juana, Octavio Paz alerts us to a fundamental characteristic of literary discourse that he finds especially pertinent to an informed approach to Sor Juana's work: silences speak.[184] What is communicated—what is written—forms a meaning-laden *chiaroscuro* with what is left unsaid; a reader who is awakened to the particular silences of a text apprehends a deeper pattern than one who takes words at their "innocent" face value. For Paz, the relationship between "*las expresas y las implícitas*" is correlated to the categories of power and prohibition: silences are evidence of enforcement.[185] In Sor Juana's case, a high degree of regimentation and bureaucratic structure connected to the religious environment of seventeenth-century New Spain placed strict boundaries around "*lo decible*"—that which could be (or was *permitted* to be) said.[186] Then as now, a text in such an environment encodes its message twice: once discursively, once subversively.

Paz's "Prologo" sensitizes us to the silences in Sor Juana's writing. The silences are related to the (threat of a) community of (potential) readers at the time of her work: "*la zona de lo que no puede decir está determinada por la presencia invisible de los lectores terribles*" ("the zone of that which cannot be said is determined by the invisible presence of terrifying readers").[187] The power to enforce silence over what can be spoken extends to that which can be written. Nowhere is the tension between what is written and what "cannot" be written stronger than in Sor Juana's *Respuesta a Sor Filotea*. Her *Respuesta* dares to enter into these places of silence and to challenge the power that demands it. Using the language of vocation, Sor Juana contends that her initial theological critique of a sermon by Portuguese Jesuit Antonio Vieira—ostensibly the presenting issue in this remarkable exchange—is due to "*este natural impulso que Dios puso en mí*": God causes her to write.

Entering the sphere which religious authority has claimed for itself—and marked as a place of silence for others—locates Sor Juana's *Respuesta* precisely at the intersection of language and power. Rhetoricians such as David Jasper, for example, explore the relationship between power and written discourse. While Paz notes especially the interplay between silence and *lo decible*, Jasper is interested in how language itself (whether explicitly rhetorical or otherwise) operates as "an entextualising process which both forms community and perhaps suggests the nature and purposes of religious community."[188] It is important to acknowledge that religious language is deployed by religious authorities to inscribe community norms: who can participate, in what way, and at what point their participation becomes unwelcome are all part of the (unseen) freight and intent of religious rhetoric.

Sor Juana's *Respuesta* is an instance of theological discourse overtly struggling with the power of the Church hierarchy and its power to enforce the norms of the religious community. Especially in light of the Bishop's assumed identity and gender, the way that language is deployed in the exchange between Sor Juana and "Sor Filotea" highlights the manner in which (as Jasper says) the "nature and purpose of the religious community" is set out, delineated, and enforced in a way that is typically less than overt.[189] Sor Juana's *Respuesta* is both explicitly and implicitly a form of transgressive rhetoric which *crosses purposes* with the community-norming power of the Bishop's office.

The exchange between the nun Sor Juana and the "nun" "Sor Filotea" is a negotiation of the nature of community, the permissibility of women's participation in theological discourse, and the way power masks itself in seemingly innocent language to enforce its strictures. These actions of power and uses of rhetoric are not limited to seventeenth-century New Spain. A wide variety of texts written during widely different historical moments evince similar dynamics. Importantly, then, an analysis of the exchange between Sor Juana and Sor Filotea has implications not only for those interested in a clear understanding of how rhetoric functioned in particular historical moments; powerful (and "masked") rhetoric operates no less in contemporary communities, particularly where gender is invoked (explicitly or implicitly) as a condition of access to discourse.

## *Rhetorical Aspects of La Respuesta*

Rhetoric as classically understood is capable of being persuasive even as it runs along lines tangential to or even opposed to the truth. Conceivably, theological discourse regarding the nature of religious communities may seek the ends of those in power rather than any sort of outcome which might change the structures of the community in favor of the disenfranchised. For just these reasons, an analysis of the nature of religious discourse and rhetoric are especially helpful in appreciating what is being negotiated in the exchange between Sor Juana and "Sor Filotea."

A contest framed as an "argument" actually works to mask the true location of power in a textual exchange. Reading a thesis set forth by rhetorician Chaim Perelman, David Jasper observes that the very act of couching negotiations in terms of an argument is the first step in hiding the true nature of a given discourse and the power beneath it:

> Rhetoric, the art of persuasion, works not from ontology but from a form of argumentation...argumentation may be powerful in its claims upon us even although its truth is evasive. We return again to Perelman's thesis that the argument works not from premise but towards consent in the community to a given thesis or theses. *Its concern is the establishment of an unavoidable authority.*[190]

Religious rhetoric guided by authoritative power is at its persuasive best when its claims are not seen as the authoritative claims that they actually are, but appear as innocent and self-evident truths. The modality of argumentation may have nothing to do with the truth, so to speak, but its employment of argumentative discourse is itself persuasive., especially if the power resident within the arguer is disguised—making its authority "unavoidable." Claims framed in argumentative terms invite further argument: by masking the true nature of the Bishop's authority, Sor Filotea effectively enhances his ability to deploy religious authority in a way that (because it is not overtly "arguing" anything from a position of power, but only "argues" from a position of a peer) is virtually incontrovertible.

The exchange between the Bishop's "Sor Filotea" and Sor Juana cannot be shown to have had a decisive outcome or effect.[191] Sor Juana ruminates on the necessity of the exchange at the outset of her *Respuesta*, trying to discern what her hypothetical silence might communicate in the face of the *Carta Atenagórica* and the *Carta de Sor Filotea* appended thereto.[192] Obviously, Sor Juana chose to engage the process, but the drama of her decision becomes a part of her *Respuesta* itself:

> I confess I was looking for a subterfuge that would allow me to evade the difficulty of responding to you. But silence is a negative thing, and although it explains much through its emphasis on not explaining, it is necessary to affix some

> brief label to it so that it is understood to be signifying silence.[193]

Bearing in mind especially Paz's insights into the nature of silence, we discover in Sor Juana's *Respuesta* a deliberate and preemptive gloss (her "brief label") on a silence that refuses to be silent. Her text is one level of her response—again, *lo decible*—and cannot be read without the concomitant silence that she calls attention to here.[194] Even if there is little hope for change in the status of women in the community of theological discourse being negotiated in this exchange, Sor Juana *chooses to enter the process*: it is necessary.

If a particular outcome is unlikely to result from a process of negotiation such as that between the nun and the "nun," readers of the exchange need to discern what else may be at stake. The negotiation is at one level about the role of women in theological discourse: Sor Juana negotiates in favor of the full inclusion of women in this (textual) community, while Sor Filotea is perhaps more cynical on the same issue. But if nothing happens to affect the status quo, where might the meaning of this exchange reside? Insofar as each letter *represents* certain aspects of each individual in written form, the letters can be read as *representatives* deployed into a framed space (created through publication). Ostensibly on duty to negotiate the boundaries which govern participation in theological discourse, these representative masks or avatars—for even Sor Juana works to maintain the suspension of actual identity in the exchange—are engaged in a rehearsal of a community's understanding of itself as involved in setting, testing, and enforcing boundaries. The exchange between the nun and the "nun" similarly gathers the variety of ways that Christian community might be construed and, in the process of "facing off," brings the loose ends of the nature of the community into an orderly construct. The documents advance like champions into the sphere of public theological discourse to contend for their own particular image of the nature of religious community.

It is not finally the outcome of the negotiation that creates meaning, but the act of encounter: this act of *facing each other* is an essential aspect and requirement for community. To remain silent would have been an abdication of a sort of communal responsibility (the requirement of a response) on Sor Juana's part. Sor Juana, of course, sees her participation in such discourse as legitimate and conducive to a desired community, while "Sor Filotea" seeks to negotiate a more ordered community, resistant to changes in the *status quo*. But a mere analysis of the positions held by each side in this debate misses the fact that the act of facing each other in theological discourse is the essential component of religious community being performed by this textual exchange.

## Masks and the Nature of Community

"Sor Filotea" is a religious authority masquerading as a sympathetic interlocutor. Bishop Fernández uses this rhetorical construct—an assumed identity *and* gender—as a written veil. Granted that words are never exactly or only what they *seem* to say, in this case the duplicitous tendency of language is leveraged to heightened effect. In light of the fact that most erudite readers of the *Carta de Sor Filotea* would have understood that it was Bishop Fernández' composition—Paz calls it "an open secret"—what use is his/her mask?[195] The motivations operating behind the Bishop's choice of persona are irrecoverable, but the very process of assuming a mask in this theological text highlights the way rhetoric works to shape religious communities. There is an ironic element in textual discourse which at once separates language from its *intended meaning* and its *implicit meaning* while still allowing a community to see itself as united in the search for unifying knowledge of the divine. In spite of the unreliability of language in the construction and convening of community, "God's inbreaking is remarked as a trace, an absolute otherness, upon the linguistic structure."[196] Imperfect language does not negate the possibility that God is present as the longed-for subject of the discourse. The masked interlocutors locked in a dialectical exchange stand as an emblem of religious community: their rhetoric never escapes the gravitational pull of irony, but the trace of the divine clings to their language and is the true constitutive element in their community of theological discourse.

Theological language operates *on the surface* according to rational propositions and *beneath the surface* as non-propositional or un-rational persuasion. In the *Respuesta*, a strong ironic sense constantly lurks behind the evident or superficial burden of the text. This ironic note that dominates the very first paragraph of the *Respuesta* as Sor Juana opens her letter with protestations as to her own worthiness to respond to "Sor Filotea." Sor Juana writes that she nearly refrained from responding, "no como el Santo [Tomás], por humilidad, sino que en la realidad es no saber algo digno de vos" ("not as Saint Thomas, through humility, but because in reality it is because [I] know nothing worthy of you").[197] In this case, the *double entendre* around "not knowing anything worthy" about "Sor Filotea" sets an ironic—even sarcastic—tone, reinforced throughout the text with similar half-concealed references to details of the actual (un-masked) scenario.

## Intimacy with the Divine: Sor Juana's Poetry of Affection

Sor Juana's self-defense in the *Respuesta* covers more than rationalistic theological discourse. She also defends her poetry, especially poetry written in an affectionate, intimate, or erotic timbre.[†*] Sor Juana rises to heights of rhetorical animation when she demands of "Sor Filotea":

---

† "Erotic" in this section refers merely to poems addressed primarily and affectionately to other individuals and does not imply sensuality. Some scholars have read Sor Juana's "love poems" as sensual, particularly biographers such as Ludwig Pflandl, who approached her work with psychoanalytical theoretical lenses.

> What harm then can there be in poetry?...If evil consists in women writing poetry, we have already seen that many women have used poetry in a praiseworthy fashion. What then is the harm in my doing so? Of course, I admit I am base and vile, but I do not believe that anyone has seen a single indecent couplet of mine.[198]

The oblique reference to "indecent couplets" raises the issue of the so-called "profane" poetry that Sor Juana wrote occasionally.[‡*] Its subject matter was aimed less at the religious community and more at the courtly community she also knew from her pre-convent days.[199] More than the chaste, careful, disembodied reflections of a professed religious, these poems (numbering about fifty, according to Paz) are fundamentally erotic.[200] Given the prevailing and tacit (if less than supportive) ambivalence toward her erotic poetry up until the point of composition of the *Respuesta*, what might lie beneath Sor Juana's decision to defend her poetry now? If Sor Juana feels the need to defend her erotic poetry, it may be because Bishop Fernández (or those with political influence over him) have been placed in a position in which (due to changes in the political climate, for example) they need emphatically to designate Sor Juana's brand of love poetry as existing outside the pale of approved religious discourse. As the authority responsible for norming participation in the religious community, the Bishop polices the boundaries of the community—and discerns the erotic, perhaps especially as it becomes associated with an individual increasingly noted for her participation in specifically theological discourse, as a threat. Poets can write erotic poetry, but as Sor Juana claims her identity as theologian—a claim heralded especially by her critique of Vieira's sermon—the content of her profane poetry calls more urgently for suppression. Such a tendency in the Church to suppress eroticism is by no means remarkable in and of itself. But when erotic poetry accompanies the coolly rational theological discourse of a theologian such as Sor Juana, it is perhaps doubly threatening: could the

‡ Latin "pro fanum," "outside the temple."

erotic discourse use theological ratiocination as a Trojan Horse to enter into the well-regulated community? The possibility may have been perceived, at least by one as politically savvy as a bishop.

To ears accustomed to the standard historiography around the Roman Catholic Church in the seventeenth century (emphasizing the Church's Inquisition and its need to control religious practice), such an exclusion of eroticism seems "natural." Like most such conventions, however, the exclusion of the erotic as a valid category for interpreting and describing religious experience is constructed and enforced by the rhetoric of those in positions of authority. In other words, there is nothing "natural" about excluding "nature" from religious discourse. For Georges Bataille (1897-1962), French philosopher, writer, and sometimes theologian, the manner and nature of the exclusion of eroticism—intimacy—from religious discourse was of great importance. Bataille argues in his *Theory of Religion* that a strictly rational or "discursive" approach to intimacy with the divine is doomed from the start: true intimacy is "dangerous" and wild, a threat to orderly society, and "cannot be expressed discursively."[201] For Bataille, "the sacred is that prodigious effervescence of life that, for the sake of duration, the order of things holds in check, and that this holding changes into a breaking loose, that is, into violence."[202]

True intimacy with the divine represents a tremendous threat to religious order as construed by authorities such as Bishop Fernández: as Sor Juana's poetry sought to escape merely "discursive" theological discourse and explore intimacy with the divine through metaphors of human intimacy, her potential to upset the highly structured religious society increased. Even though intimacy with God is a legitimate and even essential aspect of religion—to exclude it is more dangerous than to explore it—the language of intimacy is ineluctably provocative and can invite censorship. Sor Juana's love poetry, though at base representative of a theology of intimacy with the divine, brought the risk of censorship in its wake. An attempt to regulate Sor Juana's theological discourse, therefore, may have been related to her threatening intimacy with the sacred in her love poems.

By the conclusion of her *Respuesta*, Sor Juana has defended her right to write love poetry, as well as to engage theological issues as a full-fledged theologian. Simultaneously, but in a less overt fashion, she has modeled an essential component of community: engagement in its norming discourse. Although she may or may not have moved the boundaries set for the normal operation of religious community, her participation is itself significant. In fact, her participation has echoed through the centuries with persuasive and inspiring power: her theology is brilliant, beautiful, and insightful, and her engagement with the powers of church authority stands as a testimony to the importance of speaking truth to power regardless of the likelihood of effecting substantive change.

## Communal Discourse and Rhetoric: Beyond the Masks

Prosopagnosia is a medical condition which prevents affected individuals from recognizing others by their facial features. People with prosopagnosia determine others' identity through a variety of other strategies because of their inability to recognize faces. It is assumed that only a small proportion of people have prosopagnosia, perhaps only about 2% of the population.[203] Reading the exchange between Sor Juana and "Sor Filotea", however—in which rhetorical faces are deployed in a way that masks power and nearly destabilizes identity—shows how the inherent evasiveness of language makes the condition of (linguistic) prosopagnosia a virtually inevitable component of community. To the extent that the imprecision of language inheres in all human relationships, the tendency of language to play in, on, and around truth is inescapable. With language as one of the primary mediators of human interaction, there are no "face-to-face" relationships—words mask as much as they reveal. Recognition in such a community must depend on identity markers other than "faces." As in the exchange of letters between Sor Juana and "Sor Filotea," the tendency of language to conceal authority on the one hand and the desire for a daringly egalitarian and intimate community on the other creates ambiguity in communities which depend on language to carry meaning and to build relationships on the basis of recognition, commonality, and the shared identity that comes from shared experience.

If all language is rhetorical, then, what hope can we hold out for anything approximating what is intended by the ambiguous phrase "authentic community?" The language we believe we share has a mind and a face of its own, and our community life often takes place in spite of the weird tendency of language toward trick, equivocality, and unintended meaning(s). Using language to approach truth and to approach each other, we find that it slips and loses traction. In light of this reality, religious communities are best served by an awareness of the tricks language plays *and*—taking our cue from language itself—a playfulness with language of our own. Granting that discursive language will forever fail to carry us into intimacy with the sacred or with each other, why not experiment with words more, de-regiment communal theological discourse, and let divinity have more room to play in our hearts and minds?

Observing rhetoric's role in shaping communal discourse need not lead to the belief that all attempts to regulate public discourse are nefarious. There are legitimate reasons to provide structure around and within public discourse, whether political, religious, or otherwise. Adequate structuring of public discourse can actually work to enhance the engagement of vulnerable participants rather than exclude them. In fact, appreciating the way that language hides as much (or more) than it reveals can deepen our wonder at the phenomenon of community and the need to understand that community as *independent* of the language which appears to be its primary constitutive element. Ultimately, it is not language—

with all of its tricks and tendency to misbehave—which calls and holds us together within religious communities, but the desire for knowledge of the divine, clear and without mask, thoroughly un-rhetorical and yet deeply compelling.

## Religious Epistemology in Conversation

Religious knowledge is not something that exists hermetically sealed within an individual mind. It is, rather, something that is discerned and shared among others and within communities. In Sor Juana's case, her efforts toward discerning an epistemological approach which could value poetic as well as reason-based elements showed great promise. When it came to sharing her insights with others, her poetry and her drama were eminently successful and well-received. Later in her writing career, though, when her work steered toward the public presentation of theological knowledge, she ran into resistance. As difficult as it is to discern knowledge in a multi-cultural context, it can be even more difficult to articulate it. This is not necessarily because the knowledge itself is ineffable or somehow beyond expression. In Sor Juana's case, and in the case of many would-be participants in theological discourse, the challenge became one of *permission* to participate (rather than *capacity* to participate) in the larger discussion. Simply perceiving a truth and being able to articulate that truth does not automatically grant one license to participate in the sorts of conversations where such truths are negotiated.

Access to participation in a conversation is not always granted or denied in clear, overt ways. An invitation to participate—"you may"—can at the same time be accompanied by more subtle signals that convey a hidden "you may not." The way that access to important conversation is granted or denied, then, can be an elusive process to investigate. It pays to analyze how Sor Juana experienced often indirect but powerful resistance to her participation in public theological discourse. She was invited to participate, but her participation was then accompanied by subtle and not-so-subtle messages that claimed that her participation was illegitimate and undesirable.

Seeing and analyzing this phenomenon as it worked itself out in Sor Juana's career has implications for contemporary political and religious conversations (among others), since the overt messages which claim that participation is open to all are often accompanied by masked messages that work to limit participation. This dynamic was frustrating for Sor Juana especially because the criterion for denying participation was a fundamental aspect of her identity: her gender. Likewise, other personal characteristics or social locations—linguistic, cultural, or class-based—can be used to disqualify would-be participants in important conversations which they are otherwise completely qualified to enter. This is not an invitation to cynicism: it does matter, however, that instances of conversational gatekeeping are often disguised as a benign interest in the common good or (as in Sor Juana's case) tender concern for one's well-being. When the power to grant or deny access to public discourse is masked in such a way, the conversation risks the loss of valuable diversity, vitality, and perspective.

## Language and Community

Ultimately, the formation of community (thankfully) does not depend on that aspect of language which we sometimes wish it possessed: certainty. Language seems never to take anything like *certain truth* as its antecedent. The tricks of masking (and speaking from behind masks) highlights an important quality of religious discourse which brings cultures into "conversation": the metaphor of conversation emphasizes the centrality of language, but work such as Sor Juana's helps reveal the frailty of words in the face of communal participation. A model of cross-cultural encounter that appreciates the trickiness of language might adapt and come to depend on *embodiment with others* rather than *speaking with others.*

Presence may be more important than language. Cross-cultural communities often involve "language barriers"—but even when language is held in common, it remains wobbly and imprecise; accompaniment, companionship, and embodiment are surer foundations.

Sor Juana's exchange with Bishop Fernández/"Sor Filotea" through *La Respuesta* demonstrates (and employs) the tricks and subtexts that inhabit verbal inscriptions of community: words cannot build a space stable enough for honest encounter, but become part of the masking process which hides us from each other. Communities are able to engage in vital discourse because they are communities, whereas the converse may not always be similarly true: not all conversation leads to community formation. The Pauline ideal of being "known as we are known" works with the critique implied by Sor Juana in *La Respuesta* and suggests that *being* together is frequently more important than *talking* together. The challenge of cross-cultural encounter is best visualized as *presence working toward words* rather than *words working toward community.*

# Chapter 6

## Speaking Knowledge in Community: Vocation, Gender, and Participation

| | |
|---|---|
| *Estudia, arguye y enseña,* | *It is of service to the Church* |
| *y es de la Iglesia servicio,* | *that women argue, tutor, learn,* |
| *que no la quiere ignorante* | *for He Who granted women reason* |
| *El que racional la hizo.* | *would not have them uninformed.* |

—Sor Juana, #317, Villancico VI, "Santa Caterina" 1691,
trans. Margaret Sayers Peden

Sor Juana from an early age perceived that her *desear saber*—her desire to know—was a central part of her identity. She felt that she had no choice but to be led by this desire to know:

> This manner of reflection has always been my habit, and is quite beyond my will to control; on the contrary, I am wont to become vexed that my intellect makes me weary; and I believed that it was so with everyone, as well as making verses, until experience taught me otherwise; and it is so strong in me this nature, or custom, that I look at nothing without giving it further examination.[204]

The theme recurs throughout her *Respuesta a Sor Filotea*, invoked consistently to argue that her desire for knowledge is a gift (sometimes experienced as a burden) from God. As divine gift, then, it demands respect and realization, and not only as a private enterprise toward encyclopedic knowledge. Her desire for knowledge is at the root of her vocation, and vocations entail public expression. As Sor Juana increasingly exercised and eventually defended her pursuit of knowledge in the realm of public theological discourse, one of the pivotal points of controversy was related to her gender. When Bishop Fernández invoked Sor Juana's gender as among his primary concerns in his *Carta de Sor Filotea,* he revealed his sense that gender and vocation are essentially linked. In his view, gender circumscribes the realm of possible vocational options. In her response, Sor Juana picks up this argument—and argues that her gender is far less important to her vocation than the gift that she has received from God: her *desear saber,* her desire for knowledge.

## Vocation as "Calling" within Community

Sor Juana understood the notion of vocation (literally in Latin, "calling") in Christian terms, though parallels to the idea are certainly attested in other religious traditions (not to mention in secular circles). At base, vocation is the sense that individual strengths find especially appropriate expression in community. Vocation combines personal giftedness with a sense of responsibility for the common good. If vocation were to flow directly from giftedness, the task of finding one's work would be simple (at least in theory): discover your gift, discover your work. Of course, things are seldom so clear—missed (or wrong) turns, unhelpful advice, resistance (from self or others), and a host of other factors all conspire to create a sort of "noise" that can drown out the call of one's talent. The approbation of one's community can improve the odds, but approbation is not to be taken for granted: a range of responses is perhaps more typical, and may include opposition.

Nevertheless, the notion that vocation locates itself at the intersection "where [one's] deep gladness and the world's deep hunger meet" has gained considerable traction in current-day thinking about vocation, and similar ideas certainly had currency in Sor Juana's time.[205] It is compelling both for its simplicity and its apparent truth. And while drawing a direct line between a sense of one's giftedness and one's vocation may seem to rely on the relatively recent psychology of self-esteem and the logic of self-realization, it is well attested in other historical contexts when this language was unknown. While notions of giftedness may seem subjective and difficult to define, here (as in the *Respuesta*) the idea of gift is fundamentally a practice or activity which brings great subjective joy, appears to form an essential part of one's deep identity, and which is not unduly harmful to others. It is not, however, merely a way of favoring one's idea of a good time with the vocabulary of divine will. For Sor Juana, the joy of the gift is persistently accompanied by the burden which comes from faithfulness to its imperatives. It is the joy of obedience to one's nature, which is not to be confused with ease and frivolity. And it is, finally and fundamentally, linked to the needs of one's community.

Sor Juana's works were the result of precisely this sort of discernment: her loyalty to her vocation was unwavering, even though her writing on certain subjects was met with disapproval. Sor Juana is among those who, in spite of the difficulties attending the move directly from one's giftedness to an articulation and embrace of one's vocation, have hewn to this principle. She was an individual who interpreted her gift for language and learning as constitutive of her identity and allowed this identity to decide her vocation.

Sor Juana's *Respuesta a Sor Filotea* directly engages categories of giftedness (or charism, to use a related term), gender, and vocation. It can be read as an argument for vocational identity based *primarily* on giftedness. This category captures her sense of an identity rooted in a constellation of proclivities, talents, and desires which virtually demand realization. It also connotes a sort of "given-ness" or life-long presence which transcends the category of choice. In this equation, the gifts determine and are expressed through the vocation. What Sor Juana considers secondary (though not insignificant) concerns—in this case, gender roles and the authority of the Church hierarchy—cannot diminish her commitment to the practice and realization of her gift. Her argument uses her sense of joy in writing and thinking as the basis for her vocation, while simultaneously attempting to debunk the notion that her gender makes this vocation untenable.

For Sor Juana, giftedness (as discerned through the subjective experience of joy, or Buechner's "gladness") trumps other aspects of identity such as gender and societal prescriptions related to gender. And while reference to communal approbation of this subjective sense of gift are present in the *Respuesta* to lesser extent, Sor Juana's case is ultimately founded in her sense of God's role in creating her unique identity: her belief that God gave her the *desear saber* is decisive. Finding examples throughout history, Sor Juana argues that the gift is greater than the culturally conditioned strictures that seek to limit the expression of the gift:

> I find a most wise Queen of Saba, so learned that she dares to challenge with hard questions the wisdom of the greatest of all wise men, without being reprimanded for doing so, but, rather, as a consequence, to judge unbelievers. I see many and illustrious women; some blessed with the gift of prophecy, like Abigail; others of persuasion, like Esther; others with pity, like Rahab; others with perseverance, like Anna, the mother of Samuel; and an infinite number of others, with divers gifts and virtues.[206]

## Arguments from Theological Anthropology in *La Respuesta*

For Sor Juana, a gift from God is anthropologically constitutive. A gift from God which is inherent to one's identity cannot be removed without removing something basic and essential. Moreover, such a gift is given with an expectation of use, not suppression. As Grady C. Wray points out, Sor Juana is not naïve regarding the use of this principle:

> [Sor Juana] recognizes the talents God has given her. She also knows the responsibility and problems such gifts bring. She even likens the possession of God's gifts to punishment...she suggests that others should not criticize those who have received talents from God because the receipt of a benefit requires a responsible correspondence.[207]

The relative simplicity of the principle does not imply simplicity in following its logic. Nevertheless, it is clear that loyalty to a gift's imperatives is akin to loyalty to God, with disloyalty to the gift logically equivalent to disloyalty to God. This loyalty is to be maintained even in the face of difficulty.

Given Sor Juana's nuanced view of gift, then, it is important to appreciate the way in which she sets out in the *Respuesta* to prove the divine origin of her *desear saber*. It is one thing to claim that one has been given a gift from God, but how might one substantiate such a subjective claim? Her approach is autobiographical: Sor Juana demonstrates the presence of her gift for writing and thinking through a series of anecdotes from childhood, each designed to show signs of God's gift to her and her early dedication to its realization. One notable narrative focuses on events from age three, the age at which she learned to read: she had pursued her *inclinación*, she says, and had followed "one of her elder sisters to learn to read at a school for girls."[208] She recalls how she tricks this elder sister into letting her into the classroom and how "before my mother knew of it I could already read."[209] The moral of the story is that the gift for language and the desire to engage it was already present at an early age; the suggestion is that its early manifestation argues in favor of its "given-ness" rather than its later affectation. Similarly, at about the same time, Sor Juana gave up eating cheese "because [she] had heard that it made one slow of wits, for...the desire for learning was stronger that the desire for eating—as powerful as that is in children."[210] To the extent that children are unformed versions of their future adult identities, Sor Juana can argue that her nature as a child equals the nature that God intended for her. This is crucial to her understanding of vocation based on identity and nature, and she works hard to establish this point early on in the *Respuesta.*

When the seven-year-old Sor Juana realizes that there is a university in nearby Mexico City, she meets the first real resistance to her desire to feed her gift for learning and language: her mother prohibits her from "dress[ing] in boy's clothing and send[ing] me to Mexico City to live with relatives."[211] She works around this refusal by reading on her own the books owned by her grandfather, taking punishments in stride. In this anecdote is contained a principle of more general application: Sor Juana wants to show that she *cannot resist* God's gift of the *desear saber*—the desire to know. It is a river that finds a course around any obstacle, seeking a new channel when the first is blocked. When resistance to Sor Juana's foray into theology comes later, her argument retains the same contours—the need to learn and to write possesses her and cannot be stopped. It redirects itself and expresses itself, even when this expression causes Sor Juana distress. The anecdote from childhood establishes this pattern.

Soon after the young Sor Juana recognized her own gift for reading and learning, others began to perceive it, as well. Communal approbation was part of her early discernment, though it of course proved short-lived and unreliable as a vocational compass. When she did go to Mexico City, "many marveled, not so much at my natural wit, as at my memory, and at the amount of learning I had mastered at an age when many have scarcely learned to speak well."[212] The fact that others see her gift is important, but secondary. Her own realization of her *desear saber* is primary—while others may "marvel" at her precociousness, she sees her gift as part of her nature and identity. These two perceptions—one of superficial display of acumen, the other of an integral part of one's identity—will continue to operate in Sor Juana's career. What others may appreciate as her "quick wit" is, for her, wrapped up in her sense of the identity God has given her and implies the work for which she has been created.

A further intensifying anecdote finds Sor Juana well on her way to mastering Latin grammar. "So deep was my concern," she writes of her study of Latin,

> that though among women (especially a woman in the flower of her youth) the natural adornment of one's hair is held in such high esteem, I cut mine off to the breadth of some four to six fingers, measuring the place it had reached, and imposing upon myself the condition that if by the time it had again grown to that length I had not learned such and such a thing I had set for myself to learn while my hair was growing, I would again cut it off as punishment for being so slow-witted.[213]

This anecdote is remarkable especially because it contrasts two images of giftedness: the gift of physical beauty and the gift of readiness in learning. Sor Juana points out that, in her observation, women of that age are especially concerned with physical beauty and give it priority—while she ruthlessly cuts her hair if its growth outpaces her learning. Dedication to the gift of learning surpasses dedication to the accidents of gender and prescribed gender roles (here, the well-defined role of being a "young beauty"). The narrative of gender roles here has less impact on Sor Juana's sense of identity than does the narrative of intellectual giftedness.

And while Sor Juana does not argue against the idea of gender *per se*, she does place it behind other anthropological elements in working out her sense of vocation. It is a question of priority more than the deconstruction of the notion of gender itself.

At this point in the *Respuesta*, Sor Juana takes up the subject of her religious profession. Having identified her *inclinación*—her gentle euphemism for her life-controlling gift—she relates her need for suitable circumstances for its care and feeding. "Given the total antipathy for marriage," she writes, "I deemed convent life the least unsuitable."[214] Her choice was not straightforward, as some convents had stricter rules of life than others. The convent of St. Jerome emerged as a good fit; she was able to accumulate a considerable library and social circle. Even granting the relative freedom of the Hieronomite order, Sor Juana relates in the *Respuesta* that her gift chafed at the requirements of community: "once [my inclination was] dimmed and encumbered by the many activities common to Religion, that inclination exploded in me like gunpowder, proving how *privation is the source of appetite.*"[215]

By this point in her narrative, Sor Juana has clearly characterized her gift as multi-faceted: it is at once a joy and a burden. To the extent that it is a joy, she feels the need to justify or explain her gladness in study. This is accomplished through invoking the "erudition" of her spiritual parents, Saints Jerome and Paula: "it was essential that such erudite parents not be shamed by a witless daughter."[216] This is only partially convincing, by her own account, and this dual experience of the gift as both favor and difficulty leads her to regulate her realization of the gift austerely. She takes an ordered and logical approach to theology—"Queen of Science," in the language of the time—first setting herself the task of climbing "the steps of the human sciences and arts."[217] This incremental approach acknowledges both the gift and the usefulness of tradition and regulation in forming that gift. While Sor Juana is individually convinced of the need to pursue her learning, she does not go so far as to make herself a "free agent" who ignores the wisdom of tradition. The role of community—including past community in the form of tradition—is part of the process of working out one's vocation.

Sor Juana's approach privileges the gift without completely ignoring the community, but she makes it clear that her loyalty is first to learning and second to the demands of community. Left to herself, she studies; when the community is in need, she responds. This pattern limits her progress, she believes. She does her best to honor the subjects of her study in spite of myriad interruptions and the lack of a trained teacher:

> ...I undertook this great task without benefit of teacher, or fellow students with whom to confer and discuss, having for a master no other than a mute book, and for a colleague, an insentient inkwell; and in the stead of explication and exercise, many obstructions, not merely those of my religious obligations...but rather all the attendant details of living in a community: how I might be reading, and those in the adjoining cell would wish to play their instruments and sing; how I might be studying, and two servants who had quarreled would select me to judge their dispute.[218]

The resistance to the realization of her gift is substantial, giving evidence of the depth of its rootedness—it is essential to her identity, and to deny it or allow other considerations to overwhelm it is inconceivable. So compelling is this piece of her identity, and so likely to cause friction between herself and others (especially the Church, as in the context of the *Respuesta*), that she confesses her "envy" of those who have not been "plagued by my thirst for knowledge: blessed are they."[219]

The power of her gift to confer identity and to find expression becomes especially evident as Sor Juana relates an instance of attempted cessation of study. She tells of an "Abbess who believed that study was a thing of the Inquisition, who commanded me not to study."[220] This command changed Sor Juana's external behavior, but the inclination itself proved more tenacious:

> ...for though I did not study in books, I studied all the things that God had wrought, reading in them, as in writing and in books, all the workings of the universe. I looked on nothing without reflection; I heard nothing without meditation, even in the most minute and imperfect things; because as there is no creature, however lowly, in which one cannot recognize that *God made me,* there is none that does not astound reason, if properly meditated upon.[221]

The *Respuesta* points out that this irrepressible tendency to study and "meditate" is so deep as to be essential and impossible to eradicate. Sor Juana is "vexed" with this irrepressibility; her joy in learning is accompanied by difficulty—not just as a result of the circumscriptions of authority, but also due to its raw force and constancy. In one passage, she even refers to her desire for learning as *mi locura*—"my madness."

A further (and charming) example of Sor Juana's compelling gift for learning can be taken from her anecdotes around cooking. As she continues to argue that her *desear saber* is innate and irrepressible, she illustrates by telling how she has studied even the way that ingredients in the kitchen express natural laws and scientific principles. She gives a few examples: "I see that an egg holds together and fries in butter or in oil, but, on the contrary, in syrup shrivels into shreds; observe that to keep sugar in a liquid state one need only add a drop or two of water in which a quince or other bitter fruit has been soaked..."—along with a great many other similar observations.[222] She believes that the irrepressibility of her gift for learning is persuasive and suggests that its "given-ness" will not brook resistance, whether from herself or from outside. These anecdotes conclude with the oft-quoted line, "had Aristotle cooked, he would have written a great deal more."[223]

At this point in the progress of the *Respuesta*, Sor Juana begins to introduce the language of her "nature" as a synonym for her gift for learning. At the conclusion of her sequence of cooking anecdotes, she says to the Bishop-as-"Sor Filotea" "the above is sufficient to allow your discretion and acuity to penetrate perfectly and perceive my nature (*mi natural*), as well as the beginnings, the methods, and the present state of my studies."[224] The sequence here is telling: her logic proceeds from nature to vocation, from "inclination" to study and learning. More importantly, the shift from the language of the *desear saber* to the language of "nature" signals a turn toward anthropology: one's nature is essential and constitutive: not *chosen*, but *given*. Moreover, in a system with God as creator, nature is given by God. Importantly, Sor Juana makes much of God's gift of her nature as related to her *desear saber*, but does not use this same language of given-ness regarding her gender. The *desear saber* is at the core of her nature. Gender, by its exclusion from this line of argument, is relegated to a less decisive position.

The *Respuesta* ends in flurry of ironic obsequiousness, leaving the argument to stand for itself while preserving the mask of submissiveness. Sor Juana has made her argument: nature, she claims, determines vocation. Gender—and the expectations of others based on gender—do not determine vocation, since the divine imprint exists primarily in the nature of one's gift and not on gender.

## Cultural Encounter and Vocation

While the subject of gender constitutes the primary battlefield on which Sor Juana engages Bishop Fernández, it is good to keep in mind that she was also attempting to discern and express her vocation in a cross-cultural context. In the flow of cultural mixing between European and Mesoamerican understandings, effectively various versions of reality were on offer. Located between worlds, Sor Juana lived with a kind of cultural relativism. And while the vocabulary of cultural relativism and cultural construction may be recent, the principles are timeless. Living between cultures in any historical moment can give rise to something like relativism or, at any rate, the need to negotiate the claims of contrasting systems. In such a complex situation, the need for a single point of orientation is easy to appreciate. It is understandable, then, that neither gender roles nor fluctuating cultural norms exist in her thinking as decisive elements of her vocation. In the *Respuesta,* the single point she repeatedly invokes is her own nature or "inclination." It is not all that she considers, of course, but it is significant that she locates her sense of clarity in an assessment of her own nature rather than in the nature of a cultural paragon, whether gender-based or otherwise. Sor Juana, like others living with cultural complexity, finds a way to center and clarify her thinking by bringing it to the level of the known and knowable—her own identity and nature.

As much as Sor Juana's *Respuesta* lends itself to an anthropology favoring giftedness over gender as vocationally decisive, a careful reading also reveals several cautions. A system of vocational discernment based primarily on one's preferences is as dangerous as a system based overmuch on unassailable authority. Indulging the whims of the subjective self without regard to the needs of the community ignores the basic Christian imperative to see oneself as a member of a comprehensive body. In many ways Sor Juana was able to advocate for her own individual vocational discernment *precisely because* the Church hierarchy was present as structure and foil. Her *Respuesta* exists because she was provoked to write it *in engagement with community*, albeit a somewhat antagonistic representative of that community in the person of Bishop Fernández. It would be difficult to overstate the dangers of a self-centered vocational discernment if there were no communal input. Sor Juana assumes this input will be present, even if she would at the same time wish it were more favorable. In brief, then, the discernment of vocation from gift as imaged in Sor Juana's *Respuesta* must be predicated on the presence of a strong community with the ability to articulate its own needs vis-à-vis the identity of the individual seeking vocational clarity.

Sor Juana's *Respuesta* works to develop a notion of giftedness, making it synonymous with talent, nature, and (idiosyncratically) "inclination." It manifests itself early and continues to appear relentlessly throughout the various stages of life and development. Sor Juana's notion of essential giftedness (her *desear saber,* her *inclinación*) attempts to change the order of various components of human identity, placing giftedness in a place of priority *before gender and expected gender roles.* In doing so, Sor Juana establishes a principle that can hold true even when gender is replaced with other similar changeable features of identity, such as cultural difference: human nature centers on a given-ness and giftedness from God, and the realization of this gift within community is the essence of vocation. Giftedness is anthropologically constitutive. Every person is gifted. Similarly, every person is characterized by the phenomena of identity—gender, race, culture, social location, and so on. In any attempt to sort out a vocational trajectory from this mix, giftedness for Sor Juana remains central. We know (as Sor Juana clearly knew) that this is not a simple task. Nevertheless, with this principle in place, the work of discernment can find its most appropriate focus on the essence of a person, working to nurture and realize the gift that is ultimately ascribed to the generosity of God.

## Finding Sor Juana's Voice Within Feminist Movements and Critiques of Patriarchy

*Y También se que, en latín,*
*Solo a las casadas dicen*
*Úxor, o mujer, y que*
*Es común de dos lo Virgen.*
*Con que a mí no e bien mirado*
*Que como a mujer me miren,*
*Pues no soy mujer que a alguno*
*De mujer pueda servirle;*
*Y sólo se que mi cuerpo,*
*Sin que a uno u otro se incline,*
*Es neutro, o abstracto, cuanto*
*Sólo el Alma deposite.*

*I know, too, that they were wont*
*To call wife, or woman, in the Latin*
*Uxor, only those who wed,*
*Though wife or woman might be virgin.*
*So in my case, it is not seemly*
*That I be viewed as feminine,*
*As I will never be a woman*
*Who may as woman serve a man.*
*I know only that my body,*
*Not to either state inclined,*
*Is neuter, abstract, guardian*
*Of only what my Soul consigns.*

—*Poem 48 (Romances), "In Reply to a Gentleman from Peru, Who Sent Her Clay Vessels While Suggesting She Would Better Be a Man"*[225]

Sor Juana's *Respuesta* effectively argues that her gender is less important than her giftedness when it comes to working out her vocational identity and her right to participate in communal theological discourse. And this theme appears in many other places in her work, as well. Her skillful argumentation resonates with similar cases made for the inclusion of women's voices in various and varied conversations before and since her work, whether conversations around politics, intellectual discussions, religious leadership, and dozens more. Not surprisingly, growing interest in Sor Juana in the English-speaking world over the past several decades can be seen as part of a larger trend toward increased appreciation of the dynamics of patriarchy and the suppression of women's voices in literature, religion, politics, and so on. Just to name a few examples, denominational changes within mainline Protestantism, academic awareness of the complexity of gender dynamics in Western history and culture, and a renewal of interest in writing by and about women have all contributed to an era of increased attention to the work of Sor Juana.[226]

Various thinkers differ in how they pinpoint the origins of these arguments, but a notable jumping off point might be the 1792 work by Mary Wollstonecraft, *A Vindication of the Rights of Women*.[227] The emergence during the Enlightenment of the category of analysis (now more or less taken for granted) known as "individual rights" led to Wollstonecraft's appropriation of these rights and her application of them in a systematic way to issues of inequality between men and women.[228] While only one of a number of works identifying and arguing against the widespread gender bias especially in terms of the right to literary production, *A Vindication* became a standard work studied by those motivated to analyze, act, and change this reality.

The theme developed in England and made its way to the Americas, manifesting itself in the works of Emily Dickinson and others in the late nineteenth century and then with increasing force and diversity into the twentieth century. By the time Virginia Woolf published *A Room of One's Own* in 1929, the arguments in favor of women's writing and contributions to culture were more generally well-established.[229] And as political enfranchisement became a reality, women's literary and religious discourse moved increasingly into the sphere of academic study. In many ways paralleling the development of the Civil Rights movement dedicated to racial equality, curricula organized around liberal studies in the United States increasingly in the 1960s included sections or entire classes devoted to women's studies. Students and academics began to scour history for instances of women's literary agency, production, and resistance to patriarchy. Clearly, Sor Juana's life and work illustrate each of these dynamics, and her work gradually came to stand as an example of "feminist" or "proto-feminist" literature (a term used to avoid the anachronistic use of a contemporary term to apply to a historical moment in which it would not have been used).

The work of religious scholars such as Rosemary Radford Reuther and Elisabeth Schüssler Fiorenza in the 1980s and 1990s helped move the study of the feminist critique more confidently into matters of religious studies, especially investigating the foundational leadership roles that women played in the early Church and as companions of Jesus. Mainline Protestantism was affected by these critiques as they gained more traction in American culture and began to provoke an institutional response. Studies designed to recover the biblical leadership roles of women in order to argue for their right to ordination proliferated in the 1970's, and a number of denominations had lengthy and sometimes heated discussions of this possibility.

This climate of literary study, recognition of the leadership roles afforded to women in the early Church, and increasing pressure for gender equality in various mainline Protestant denominations (to say nothing of the same debates within the Roman Catholic Church) combined to create an ideal environment for renewed investigation of Sor Juana. She was at once religious and disruptive of patriarchy, at once courageous and creative, and seemed to "lengthen" the trajectory of feminist critique by providing an instance deep within the seventeenth century. And while writers such as Margaret Fell (1614-1702) and Aphra Behn (c. 1640-1689), among others, had broached the subject of gender justice either prior to or simultaneously with Sor Juana, Sor Juana is particularly American (even in spite of her orientation toward a largely Spanish audience). This makes her stand out. Scholars of gender bias and its dynamics found (and find) in Sor Juana an early example of the essential features of feminist critique which included not only implicit but explicit analysis of patriarchy. Because the themes of her life and work dovetailed so precisely with many of the concerns of feminist scholars and their allies, she appeared on the American academic horizon as an ideal subject for these studies. This is not to say that other aspects of her work went unnoticed—it is merely to indicate the contours of the academic landscape which generated interest in her life and work.

Reading Sor Juana's work for insights into the dynamics of gender as negotiated within literary and theological texts requires care: one must resist the temptation to see Sor Juana merely as an early proponent of something like modern-day feminism. This temptation is understandable, of course, since Sor Juana's *Respuesta* resonates so clearly with many of the insights and concerns of feminism. Michelle A. González, however, includes a number of cautions regarding this similarity. González acknowledges that Sor Juana scholarship is right to read her as unusually perspicacious regarding gender issues: "Sor Juana's recognition of the social construction of gender is what distinguishes her from other Baroque figures."[230] And while some scholars are "wary" of labeling Sor Juana a feminist *per se*, "feminism is the most adequate term to denote the struggle for the equality of men and women in her work."[231] Further, scholars such as Electa Arenal and Amanda Powell note that Sor Juana "argue[s] not only on her own behalf, but on behalf of all women."[232] Nevertheless, González is finally reluctant to name Sor Juana a "feminist" writer because "[Sor Juana] does not have either the systemic analysis or the link with a broader social movement that defines feminism."[233]

Gillian Ahlgren's *Introduction* to the preeminent English language anthology of Sor Juana's works, translated and edited by Pamela Kirk Rappaport, notes the way in which an interest in feminist literature and critique bolstered interest and interpretation of Sor Juana's life and texts. The fact that Rappaport's edition is included in "The Classics of Western Spirituality" series is already an indication of the ascendency of Sor Juana scholarship, buoyed in large part by the dynamic of feminism and the influential promotion of Octavio Paz in 1982 (appearing in 1988 in English). The *Respuesta a Sor Filotea* is indeed an "eloquent defense of the role and place of women as authoritative religious teachers"—and depends on Sor Juana's use of biblical and traditional material, often read against the grain of patriarchy in persuasive ways.[234] She bases her main points on her sense from an early age that she was "created" with a passion for learning and reading, graced with this charism from God. She clearly saw her natural inclination toward learning as fundamentally vocational, linked to a "call" that she was obliged to pursue. This argument uses categories of a "universal humanity" similar to those developed by Bartolomé de las Casas, whose work a century earlier had used universality to argue for the humane treatment of the Amerindians. Sor Juana uses a similar strategy to argue for her essential sameness with men called to a vocation of learning and writing, and makes a case based on her charism and obligation to her vocation. Her gender is not a disqualification of her vocation because she is, at base, on equal anthropological footing as a man given the same vocation. Gender is a non-constitutive category, while giftedness is constitutive. What we might now call her "self" (though Rousseau had yet to develop the notion of the individual as we know it today) was essentially un-gendered and therefore not only free to but *obliged* to pursue her vocation. Sor Juana cites the examples throughout history of other notable women who were praised for their contributions to the Christian faith, among them Paula herself—the namesake of her convent in Mexico City. She also reinterprets Paul's admonition that "women should keep silent" and not pursue a teaching role.[235]

The *Respuesta* goes on to develop these themes in a variety of ways, but her prose defense of the rights of women to learn, study, and write is not the sole source of this line of thinking. Before Sor Juana wrote her more discursive "defense," she was already extremely well known for her many *Devotional exercises*—and especially those related to the Blessed Virgin Mary. Sor Juana wrote a number of novenas and works designed to accompany the Rosary which highlighted Mary's role not only in Jesus' life but in the life of the Church. Even before the Immaculate Conception of Mary—the idea that Mary's own conception in the womb was free from the effects of original sin—was ensconced by papal decree as doctrine, Sor Juana was extremely devoted to this belief and clearly indicated as much in her devotional poems.

The idea of Mary's birth free from sin parallels Jesus' own purity, with the idea that his temptations never led him to sin already a commonplace of theological belief at the time. And while the cult of devotion to Mary was a common feature of Counter-Reformation spirituality—seen as a "test" of one's resistance to Protestantism, in which Marian devotion was suppressed—Sor Juana's version of this devotion is notable for its robustness. She clearly gives a very high theological and spiritual role to Mary. While this may not constitute a critique of patriarchy, it does foreground the role of the feminine in religion. It can therefore be read as a complement to Sor Juana's later prose defense of women and their active role in religious discourse. It might be argued that Sor Juana's use of Mary plays into contemporary ways of controlling women by establishing unattainable ideals which none could hope to achieve. Nevertheless, scholars who search Sor Juana's works for evidence of her basic commitments to female agency in religious matters find plausible support for this thesis in her devotional works.

The blunt fact of Sor Juana's silence after her defense of women's rights could conceivably be used to illustrate the very real risks of speaking up on behalf of the disenfranchised. It is possible to read her silence as evidence of the power of patriarchy to suppress any voices raised to challenge it. In fact, however, no decisive reading of Sor Juana's silence has yet been proposed, partly due to lack of documentary evidence, but also and perhaps primarily because of the competing ideological interests held among interpreters of the silence. In view of the fact that no proof can be marshaled to support a definitive interpretation of Sor Juana's silence, students of Sor Juana are forced to base their interpretations on little more than speculation. In spite of this dearth of hard evidence, though, various streams of feminist interpretation have emerged. It has already been noted that some see her silence as a temporary period of recharging in preparation for (some believe) even greater freedom. She was, after all, in the process of rebuilding her library when she died in 1695. On the other hand, some interpret the silence as either defeat or capitulation.

Her earliest biographer, Diego Calleja, clearly saw in the silence a return to appropriately spiritual concerns.[236] This reading has met significant resistance, largely because the commitments that Sor Juana displays throughout her literary and religious career—commitments to the active role of women in religious and theological discourse—persisted up to her death and would likely have reemerged had her life lasted longer. Many see her silence as strategic and temporary. It also seems to reverse the pattern established by the exchange between Sor Juana and Bishop Fernández in the *Carta Atenagórica, Carta del Sor Filotea,* and the *Respuesta a Sor Filotea.* Nevertheless, by removing herself from this dialogue, Sor Juana may have been claiming her right to choose her interlocutors and the conversations she wished to engage. Further, she may have been subverting the power that had moved her from poetry and drama to theological prose, a literary voice which up to that point she had not developed publicly. This is speculative, of course, but so are other readings of the silence. Given that Sor Juana was persistently driven by and faithful to her *desear saber,* and given her clear commitments to women's rights in her *Respuesta,* it seems unlikely that a final act of attempted suppression would be more effective than the countless (if more subtle) attempts to suppress her had previously been. What's more, the abruptness of her alleged conversion is suspicious: she had been consistently (since childhood) stubbornly dedicated to her desire for knowledge, and it seems unlikely that such an iron will would capitulate even in the face of serious consequences. Her literary and theological trajectory was by then well established, and she clearly had the theological abilities and awareness to defend her points and principles. Her apparent renunciation of her work and her very self-identity would enter this trajectory as a sudden and unexpected conversion, hardly characteristic of her previous behavior.

A final image that has emerged in more recent scholarship may lend credence to this interpretation of her final silence as a temporary retrenchment before further writing: an inventory of her possessions, discovered in the twentieth century and regarded as authentic, shows that Sor Juana was gradually rebuilding her beloved library and was in possession of many "bundles" of manuscripts—including recent works.[237] This suggests that she was in fact returning to her established patterns of reading, learning, and writing—and though this material was not published, it may well have been in preparation for some level of circulation. In light of the fact that from childhood Sor Juana was *driven* by her desire to learn and write, it seems improbable that a final effort on the part of those with authority over her would silence her.

## Sor Juana's Proto-Feminism in Context

Finding Sor Juana's place within the general trajectory of feminist or proto-feminist writing is important not simply as a means of identifying some of her concerns in shorthand. Concerns for gender justice, rather, are important in regard to the way in which gender has functioned within religious history and theological discourse more generally, well into the present. Religious institutions continue to wrestle with the statistical fact that most theological activity has been undertaken by men. Even highly specific elements of Sor Juana's critique survive into the current conversation—we hear echoes, for example, of her ability to see the problems that arise when rules within church discourse are inconsistently applied:

> If [the church] wish[es] that the prohibition of the Apostle

> [Paul] be applied transcendentally—that not even in private are women to be permitted to write or study—how are we to view the fact that the Church permitted a Gertrude, a Santa Teresa, a Saint Birgitta, the Nun of Agreda, and so many others, to write?[238]

Calling attention to such logical gaps continues to be a strategy within various streams of feminist critique of theological discourse. And though Sor Juana's voice at the time was among only a very few, current analysis of the disparity between men and women in communal theological discourse is represented by an immense and varied body of work. We find an example of the way this conversation has continued (yet often failed to progress) in the reflections of Anna Karin Hammar, whose "After Forty Years: Churches in Solidarity with Women?" reviews the level of participation of women in the World Council of Churches.[239] Her essay attempts to measure the degree to which women have been able to enter into the various projects of the Ecumenical Movement, which represents the legacy of a good deal of Protestant theological and vocational thinking since 1910.

In clear harmony with Sor Juana's theoretical trajectories, Hammar argues that women's participation in church dialogue is "not just 'extras' or a 'social programme', but integral to the life of the churches, the WCC [World Council of Churches] and the ecumenical movement as a whole. Women's absence from decision-making structures is *an obstacle to church unity,* the Nairobi Assembly stated."[240] As with Sor Juana in the epigraph to this chapter, Hammar sees that the church is itself diminished when the gifts and charismata of women are denigrated, ignored, or proscribed.

When Hammar turns her considerations to a section on "Women's perspectives and the gifts of the Spirit," it is almost as if the spirit of Sor Juana takes control of her pen:

> ...we can interpret what happens [when women are includ-

> ed in church dialogue] through the New Testament concept of charismata. Charismata are gifts of the Sprit given to persons in the community for its upbuilding. When women and men in the community share and act according to the insights, concerns and commitments given them, these are manifestations of the Spirit for the common good (1 Corinthians 12:7; cf. Ephesians 4:12).

While reading a passage such as this in Hammar's essay, it is important to keep clearly in view the way Sor Juana used arguments from anthropology and the notion of "giftedness"—clearly resonant with the idea of charismata as employed by Hammar. Sor Juana was convinced that her *desear saber* or "desire to know" and to participate in theological discourse was her God-given charism. As such, it could not be ignored without cost to the community as a whole. Reading Sor Juana's *Respuesta* in tandem with Hammar's evaluation of women's participation in the WCC allows the strengths of each genre to reflect and magnify those of the other. Where Hammar is concerned with the practical and statistical manifestations of women's progress in the ecumenical movement and in the church more generally, Sor Juana is concerned primarily with the theoretical underpinnings which show how such participation is good for the *community as a whole*—not simply for the women included in the conversation.

The way in which Sor Juana and Karin Hammar analyze women's participation in church dialogue is fundamentally a question of ecclesiology: how can the church be constructed and constituted in such a way that the gifts (charismata) of each are used to the building up of the whole? A further ecclesiological reflection centered on the participation of women in the church maybe found in the work of Irja Askola, whose essay "Turning Means Returning: The Assembly Theme and the Churches' Solidarity with Women."[241] Askola is convinced that nothing less than the understanding of the ecclesia is at stake in any consideration of the role of women in the church: "...there has been a shift from a justice approach (social ethics) to an ecclesiological approach. We have entered into the heart of theology, challenging the self-understanding of the church and dealing with its very nature."[242] In a similar vein as Sor Juana, then, Askola sees that the question of the participation of women in church and theological dialogue is not essentially about *women* but about the *church per se*. Sor Juana continually refers her arguments back to the identity of God, who gives gifts to the church *through people*—not in an abstract way.

A further point of contact between present-day religious discourse and the work of Sor Juana is present when Askola considers the way that "Women's experience [is seen as] marginal."[243] As a nun in a convent, sequestered and placed in a metaphorically marginal place, Sor Juana was intimately familiar with the bracketing of women's experience and efforts to contain and isolate women from the larger context of church and society. And just as in Sor Juana's time the main tool used to keep women outside of the principle spheres of theological discourse, so for Askola does "language" become "one of the most powerful instruments excluding women—both the language of church law and the vocabulary of the liturgy."[244] Language and the verbal content of theological discourse is often used to create a space which is governed be unwritten but nevertheless enforced rules for participation, which is why rhetorical analysis is such a useful tool in dismantling the constructs of patriarchy. Sor Juana's critique of Vieira's sermon (*La Carta Atenagórica)* was her entry into this circumscribed discursive space, and she of course bore the consequences of this transgression. In Askola's assessment, this same process of creating a circumscribed space which cannot be entered by women is created and maintained through language—and can therefore only be dismantled with increased attentiveness to how language is used.[245]

Thus it is clear that the challenge to patriarchy represented by the work of Sor Juana Inés de la Cruz is in continuity with present-day concerns around the participation of women in theological and communal religious dialogue. Sor Juana's efforts to deconstruct the proscriptions against women's participation in theological discourse in her *Respuesta a Sor Filotea* make excellent companion pieces to more recent efforts and understanding and challenging a similar dynamic in contemporary church practice. And while scholars such as Michelle González are cautious about using the term "feminist" to describe Sor Juana due to the potentially anachronistic nature of such a label, it is clear that Sor Juana is in direct continuity with the concerns around feminism and gender justice as currently understood and discussed. As such, her work provides a valuable locus for reflection on the degree to which a critique of patriarchy within church structures has been efficacious—and provides a good indication of the contours of future discussion, as well.

# Conclusion

*Our history has followed no single unbroken pattern—the straight line of the evolutionists, the zigzag of the dialecticians, of the circle of the neoplatonists. Our history has been a discontinuous process of fits and starts: at times a dance, at others a lethargy interrupted by a sudden violent awakening… In the case of Mexico, pre-Columbian multiplicity must be added to Spanish: like the Spain of Charles V, the Mexico of Montezuma was a mixture of many societies, tongues, and nations. For all these reasons, eras and styles do not pass in Hispanic countries; they exist side by side, nourishing and devouring one another.*[246]

--Octavio Paz, *Sor Juana: The Traps of Faith*

## Sor Juana as Companion in Cultural Encounter

Octavio Paz here effectively captures the dizzying mix of cultural, political, and religious forces that surrounded Sor Juana. Her cultural context was not settled, but was rather marked by the constant interaction of symbols, groups, and individuals from every conceivable background. This chaotic cultural milieu has much in common with our own, which is also characterized by this sort of perpetual jostling among cultures and their images, symbols, and allegiances.

Sor Juana's ability to create a theopoetic space between cultures makes her an ideal companion for all of us today who live in a globalized and cosmopolitan world where cultural encounter is increasingly the norm. We meet people from all over the world. We discover that differences are more than superficial—the differences between cultures penetrate right to the heart of our ways of knowing reality, understanding our roles within communities, and seeking access to the Divine. What's more, the political conversations that crowd our public lives frequently feature the animosity and controversy that misunderstood cultural encounter can provoke. The health of our individual relationships and our public political and religious discourse depends on a careful understanding of both the promise and the risks present in cultural encounters. Discerning a way to allow the calm unfolding of cultural encounter in such a way that its promise outweighs its problems demands that we seek support and clarity from insightful voices, both past and present.

This book has presented Sor Juana's life and work as just such an accompanying presence. Her location between cultures allowed her to reflect on and convey in her work a hybridized and even harmonized vision of what it might be like to live together with others in the midst of difference. And yet her attempts at harmonization are never facile or naïve: she is fully aware of the chaotic and violent nature of the encounter between European and Mesoamerican cultures, and she understands the power differentials that add yet another layer of complexity to cultural encounters both large and small. These power differentials accompany modern-day cultural encounters just as insidiously as they did 400 years ago, and observing Sor Juana's treatment of this dynamic can inform our work still.

In addition to her insights into the dynamics of culture, Sor Juana was equally well positioned to analyze and critique the ways that gender identity was (and still is) used to limit the realization of vocational goals and participation in communal discourse. She saw how arguments based on gender identity could be marshaled by powerful individuals and groups to prevent or curtail access to important spheres of public political and theological discourse and generally to create resistance to those whose differences make their participation in such conversations a threat to established norms. Sor Juana also saw how the skillful use of rhetoric can mask these power plays, making proscriptive gender roles seem "natural" or "given." Sor Juana's own rhetorical tactics ably dismantled these arguments in her own time and sensitize us to the role rhetoric plays in current negotiations of public speech. Sor Juana's strategy for addressing and dismantling these arguments was to demonstrate that her *desear saber*—her desire for knowledge—was written into her identity by her Creator and therefore was not subject to the whims and supposed rules of human institutions. Her identity leads to her vocation, and the permission of others is secondary and even in some ways irrelevant. Others in our communities may help us clarify our identity, since no one lives or grows in a vacuum. Nevertheless, Sor Juana argues that because she does not need Church permission to be herself, she does not need the Church's permission to live into the Self that God has created her to be. Her *desear saber*—the deepest and most enduring element of her personal makeup—is the central consideration in her exercise of her vocation. This upends the Church's proscriptions around gender roles and is clearly an early indication of the trajectory that the critique and conversation that we now know as feminism would eventually take.

The challenges of understanding cultural difference and the dynamics of contested norms around gender roles are just as much a part of our public discourse as they were when Sor Juana was writing in the seventeenth century. It is both important and exciting to visit her in her time and place—located between worlds, gifted with an intense and incisive gaze, and a tremendous writerly gift—and to see how her life and work inform our current situations and conversations. The cultural encounter between European and Mesoamerican worlds—the encounter that she embodied and observed—is still active and provocative, as current controversies around immigration abundantly illustrate. Meeting

Sor Juana in her life and works helps us see today's controversies in the light of history and reveals the long arc that this conversation has had over the centuries—it is not a recent development, and there are clearly no easy answers. Likewise, the ongoing struggle to achieve clarity around the role of gender identity in vocation and public discourse represents the present manifestation of a longstanding conversation. Sor Juana was an unusually perceptive and courageous participant in precisely this conversation, making her works relevant and essential.

The controversies around culture, gender, and distinct ways of knowing are our cultural inheritance, and they provide substantial challenges. But this inheritance does not arrive simply as a tangle of impossible knots: it also arrives with wise, insightful, and discerning voices from the same past that creates our present. Sor Juana's voice was among the most prescient and perceptive of her own time. And the richness of her gifts is no less valuable today than it was when it rose with clarity amid the controversies of her own day.

# Notes

1. Margaret Sayers Peden, trans., *Sor Juana Inés de la Cruz: Poems: A Bilingual Anthology* (Tempe, Arizona: Bilingual Press/Editorial Bilingüe, 1985), 3-5.

2. Alan S. Trueblood, trans., *A Sor Juana Anthology* (Cambridge, Massachusetts, and London: Harvard University Press, 1988), 2.

3. Pamela Kirk Rappaport, trans., *Sor Juana Inés de la Cruz: Selected Writings*. With a Preface by Gillian T. W. Ahlgren. New York: Paulist Press, 2005, 7.

4. Rappaport, *Selected Writings*, 8.

5. Ibid, 8.

6. Ibid, 9.

7. Rosalva Loreto López, "Leer, contar, cantar y escribir. Un acercamiento a las prácticas de la lectura conventual." Puebla de los Ángeles, México, siglos XVII y XVIII, Estudios de Historia Novohispana 23, (2000): 67-95.

8. The most succinct version of this chain of events may be found in Rappaport's *Sor Juana Inés de la Cruz: Selected Writings*, pp. 20-24; helpful versions with more interpretive material are found in Trueblood's *A Sor Juana Anthology* (pp. 7-10) and Peden's *Sor Juana Inés de la Cruz: Poems, Protest, and a Dream* (pp. xi-xix).

9. Pamela Kirk (Rappaport), "Christ as Divine Narcissus: A Theological Analysis of 'El Divino Narciso' by Sor Juana Inés de la Cruz," Word & World XII, 2 (Spring 1992): 147.

10. Schreiter, *Local Theologies*, 39-74.

11. Margaret Sayers Peden, *Poems, Protest, and a Dream* (New York, New York: Penguin Books, 1997), 232, 233.

12. Carlos Fuentes, *The Buried Mirror: Reflections on Spain and the New World* (Boston: Houghton Mifflin Company, 1992), 235.

13. These instances and a host of smaller (yet still expensive) conflicts are narrated in great detail in Henry Kamen, *Spain, 1469-1714: A Society of Conflict,* 3d ed. (Harlow, UK: Pearson Education LTD, 2005).

14. Peter Pierson, *The History of Spain* (Westport, Connecticut: Greenwood Press, 1999), 30.

15. Ibid., 23.

16. Roger Collins, *Early Medieval Spain: Unity in Diversity, 400-1000* (London: Macmillan Press, 1995), 159.

17. Eduardo Manzano Moreno, "Christian-Muslim Frontier in Al-Andalus: Idea and Reality," in *The Arab Influence in Medieval Europe*, eds. Dionisius A. Agius and Richard Hitchcock (Reading, England: Ithaca Press, 1994), 86. Italics mine.

18. Fuentes, *Mirror*, 63.

19. Fuentes, *Mirror*, 63-62.

20.

J. N. Hillgarth, *The Visigoths in History and Legend* (Toronto: Pontifical Institute of Medieval Studies, 2009), 119-160.

21. Fuentes, *Mirror*, 63.

22. Collins, *Early Medieval Spain*, 60-66.

23. Fuentes, *Mirror*, 63.

24. Ibid., 29-30.

25. John Edwards, *Ferdinand and Isabella: Profiles in Power* (London: Pearson Education Limited, 2005), 48.

26. J. H. Elliott, *Imperial Spain: 1469 – 1716* (New York: St. Martin's Press, 1964), 34.

27. Edwards, *Profiles*, 48-56.

28. Edwards, *Profiles*, 173.

29. Fuentes, *Mirror*, 81.

30. See especially Kamen, *Spain, 1469-1714*, 57-60. A fascinating excerpt from Colón's report is included in Klaus Koschorke, Frieder Ludwig, and Mario Delgado, eds., *A History of Christianity in Asia, Africa, and Latin America, 1450-1990: A Documentary Sourcebook* (Grand Rapids, MI: William B. Eerdmans Publishing Company, 2007), 277-278.

31. Elliott, *Imperial Spain*, 47.

32. Fuentes, *Mirror*, 110.

33. Fuentes, *Mirror*, 114.

34. Alejandra Moreno Toscano, "The Spiritual Conquest," in Daniel Cosío Villegas, ed., *A Compact History of Mexico*, 3rd ed. (México, DF: El Colegio de México, 2006), 52-56.

35. Virgilio P. Elizondo, *La Morenita: Evangelizer of the Americas* (San Antonio, TX: MACC, 1980), 68, 74.

36. For a more thorough account, see especially Elizondo, *La Morenita*, 75-81.

37. Fuentes, *Mirror*, 253 & ff.

38. Rosario Villari, "The Rebel," in *Baroque Personae,* ed. Rosario Villari, trans. Lydia G. Cochrane (Chicago: University of Chicago Press, 1995), 103; Fuentes, *Mirror,* 124-126.

39. Koschorke, Ludwig, and Delgado, eds., *Sourcebook,* 285-286.

40. Elliott, *Spain 1500-1700,* 25.

41. Ibid., 25, 26.

42. Enrique Dussel, *A History of the Church in Latin America: Colonialism to Liberation* (Grand Rapids, MI: William B. Eerdmans Publishing Company, 1981), 49.

43. Toscano, "Conquest," 53.

44. Justo L. González, *The Story of Christianity: Volume 1, The Early Church to the Dawn of the Reformation* (New York, NY: Harper-SanFrancisco, 1984), 381.

45. Peter Bakewell, "Conquest after the conquest: Spanish domination in America," in *Spain, Europe, and the Atlantic World: Essays in Honour of John H. Elliott,* Richard L Kagan and Geoffrey Parker, eds. (Cambridge, UK: Cambridge University Press, 1995), 301.

46. Ibid., 301.

47. Decades of debate regarding the anthropological status of the Mesoamerican peoples culminated in a famous debate at Valladolid in 1551, considered in greater detail later.

48. See the discussion above of Isabella's 1503 letter.

49. Toscano, "The Viceroyalty," 57.

50. Toscano, "The Viceroyalty," 57-62.

51. Toscano, "The Viceroyalty," 57-62.

52. Ibid., 59-60.

53. Asunción Lavrin, "Seventeenth-Century New Spain: A Historical Overview," in Bergmann and Schlau, eds., *Approaches,* 28-29.

54. Dussel, *History,* 47-55.

55. Ibid., 55-58.

56. Rappaport, *Selected Writings,* 8.

57. Asunción Lavrin, *Brides of Christ: Conventual Life in Colonial Mexico* (Stanford, CA: Stanford University Press, 2008), 1 & ff.

58. Electa Arenal and Stacey Schlau, eds., *Untold Sisters: Hispanic Nuns in their own Works,* rev. ed. (Albuquerque, NM: University of New Mexico Press, 2010), 2-6.

59. Stephanie Kirk, "Power and Resistance in the Colonial Mexican Convent," in Bergmann and Schlau, eds., *Approaches,* 49-52.

60. Catherine Boyle, "Sor Juana in Text and in Performance: Confronting Meaning," in Bergmann and Schlau, eds., *Approaches,* 144-152.

61. Octavio Paz, Sor Juana: Or, The Traps of Faith (Cambridge, MA: The Belknap Press of Harvard University Press, 1988), 249.

62. Henry Kamen, *Spain, 1469-1714: A Society of Conflict* (Harlow, UK: Pearson Education Limited, 2005), 189.

63. Discalced means "unshod," which indicated the more ascetical strain of any given order.

64. Williston Walker, *A History of the Christian Church*, 4th ed. (New York: Charles Scribner's Sons, 1985), 513.

65. Walker, *History,* 507.

66. Ibid., 513.

67. Fuentes, *Mirror*, 187-190.

68. Walker, *History,* 513.

69. The Inquisition in Spain can be traced to a bull granted by Pope Sixtus IV in November 1478, and differed from the more general phenomenon of "enquiries" into heresy in Europe primarily in that it was designed to discover unorthodoxy among the Jewish *Conversos* or converts to Christianity, whereas the more general pattern in other areas was to root out tendencies which eventually became Protestantism. According to Henry Kamen, the hidden purpose of the Inquisition in Spain was "to eliminate Semitic culture from official Catholicism"—which led to many *Conversos* fleeing from places of strong Inquisition presence, thus exacerbating Spain's depopulation and economic stress. Kamen, *Spain, 1469-1714,* 40-48.

70. Kamen, *Spain, 1469-1714*, 195.

71. Walker, *History,* 513.

72. Rappaport, *Selected Writings*, 268.

73. Electa Arenal and Stacey Schlau, eds., *Untold Sisters: Hispanic Nuns in their Own Works,* rev. ed. (Albuquerque, NM: University of New Mexico Press, 2010), 9-11.

74. Rappaport, *Selected Writings*, 9.

75. Ibid., 33.

76. Arenal and Schlau, *Sisters,* 9-11.

77. Of many treatments of this subject, the pioneering work is that of Gerard Cox Flynn, "The Alleged Mysticism of Sor Juana Inés de La Cruz," *Hispanic Review* 28, no. 3 (July 1, 1960): 233–244.

78. José Antonio Maravall, *Culture of the Baroque: Analysis of a Historical Structure*, Terry Cochran, trans. (Minneapolis, MN: University of Minnesota Press, 1986), 11.

79. Peden, *Poems,* vi-vii, 77-129.

80. Rappaport, *Selected Writings*, 286.

81. Elias L. Rivers, "Sor Juana's *Dream*: In Search of a Scientific Vision," in *Approaches to Teaching the Works of Sor Juana Inés de la Cruz,* Emilie L. Bergmann and Stacey Schlau, eds. (New York: MLA, 2007), 127.

82. Noted by many authors; cf. Ilan Stavans, "Introduction" in Peden, *Poems,* xx.; Paz, *Traps,* 175-178. Kircher was a prolific author who spent most of his productive years living in Rome. He believed that "in Egyptian civilization he had found the universal key for deciphering all the enigmas of history" (Paz, *Traps,* 166). Kircher's influence on Sor Juana is seen distinctly in her *Primero Sueño* and, according to Paz, amounts to a "superimposition of facts, ideas, and fantasies" as well as a "glimpse" of "vast territories that stretched beyond the boundaries drawn by the Church" (Paz, *Traps,* 176-177).

83. An excellent recent consideration of this question can be found in Lisa D. Powell, *Inconclusive Theologies: Sor Juana Inés de La Cruz, Kierkegaard, and Theological Discourse* (Macon, GA: Mercer University Press, 2013).

84. Angel del Río, *Historia de la Literatura Española: Desde los Orígenes hasta 1700,* rev. ed. (New York: Holt, Rinehart and Winston, 1963), 398-399.

85. Marsha Collins, *The* Soledades, *Góngora's Masque of the Imagination* (Columbia and London: University of Missouri Press, 2002), 2.

86. Fuentes, *Mirror,* 200-210.

87. Stavans, "Introduction," xxxi.

88. Ibid.

89. Notable studies relating the Baroque to cultural hybridity and multiculturalism include several by Mabel Moraña, as well as especially Juan Luis Suárez and Estefanía Olid-Peña, "Hispanic Baroque: A Model for the Study of Cultural Complexity in the Atlantic World," *South Atlantic Review* 72, no. 1 (January 1, 2007): 31–47.

90. Yolanda Martínez-San Miguel, "Colonial No More: Reading Sor Juana from a Transatlantic Perspective," in Bergmann and Schlau, eds., *Approaches,* 88-90.

91. Ibid., 58-59.

92. Asunción Lavrin, "Historical Overview," in Bergmann and Schlau, *Approaches,* 32-34.

93. An account of these competitions and the way they helped "transplant" Spanish literary tastes into New Spain may be found in Paz, *Traps,* 54-59. A brief note on "Poetry Contests" is also included in Jennifer L. Eich, "Women's Spiritual Lives: The History, Politics, and Culture of Religious Women and Their Institutions in Colonial Society," in Bergmann and Schlau, eds., *Approaches,* 62.

94. Koschorke, Ludwig, and Delgado, eds., *Sourcebook,* 282-295; Dussel, *History,* 49-55; García-Rivera, *St. Martin,* 45-57.

95. Odina E. González and Justo L. González, *Christianity in Latin America: A History* (New York, NY: Cambridge University Press, 2008), 43-46.

96. García-Rivera, *St. Martin,* 45.

97. García-Rivera, *St. Martin,* 45-57.

98. "Sepúlveda relied heavily on a previous argument used by the Scottish theologian John Mair. Mair argued that Aristotle's natural slave, a being possessing a mind but not in control of it, could be applied as a category to describe the new barbarians, the Amerindians" (García-Rivera, *St. Martin,* 48).

99. García-Rivera, *St. Martin,* 48-49.

100. Ibid., 48.

101. García-Rivera, *St. Martin,* 50-53.

102. Ibid., 52.

103. Ibid.

104. Stavans, "Introduction," in Peden, *Poems,* xxv.

105. Vieira was "considered one of the great prose writers of his century, [and] he was widely read and discussed in Spain and its domains" (Paz, *Traps,* 389). Reading and discussing Vieira's works, then, was a well-established stream of theological discourse, making Sor Juana's entry into that stream all the more significant and ineluctably public.

106. Lisa Vollendorf, "Across the Atlantic: Sor Juana, La Respuesta, and the Hispanic Women's Canon," in Bergmann and Schlau, eds., *Approaches,* 95-102.

107. Ilan Stavans, "Introduction," in Peden, *Poems,* xxviii.

108. A succinct and helpful discussion of the term "Mexican" as applied to Sor Juana may be found in Michelle González, "Sor Juana Inés de la Cruz: Latin American Church Mother," *Perspectivas 9* (Fall

2005): 9-24, and its companion article in the same issue, Yolanda Martínez-San Miguel, "Response to Michelle González," 25-37.

109. Stephanie Merrim, "The 'Mexican' Sor Juana," in Bergmann and Schlau, eds., *Approaches,* 77-78, 83-85.

110. Gloria Anzaldúa develops the category of *nepantla* in many of her works. See especially "Chicana Artists: Exploring *Nepantla, el Lugar de la Frontera,*" in Antonia Darder and Rodolfo D. Torres, eds., *The Latino Studies Reader: Culture, Economy & Society* (Malden, MA: Blackwell Publishers, 1998), 163-169.

111. Fuentes, *Mirror,* 82.

112. Lavrin, "Historical Overview," 34-36.

113. Lavrin, "Historical Overview," 33.

114. Fuentes, *Mirror,* 126, 171.

115. Among many descriptive and interpretive works on the Guadalupe event, see especially the early and influential work of Virgilio Elizondo, *La Morenita: Evangelizer of the Americas* (San Antonio, TX: MACC, 1980).

116. Toscano, "The Viceroyalty," 53.

117. Dussel, *History,* 47-58.

118. Margaret Sayers Peden, *Poems, Protest, and a Dream* (New York, New York: Penguin Books, 1997), 204, 205.

119. Miguel León-Portilla, "Those Made Worthy by Divine Sacrifice: The Faith of Ancient Mexico," in Gary H. Gossen, ed., *South and Meso-American Native Spirituality: From the Cult of the Feathered Serpent to the Theology of Liberation* (New York, NY: The Crossroad Publishing Company, 1997), 243.

120. Elizondo, *La Morenita,* 13-15.

121. Ibid., 15.

122. Ibid., 60-62.

123. Miguel León-Portilla, "Those Made Worthy by Divine Sacrifice: The Faith of Ancient Mexico," in Gary H. Gossen, ed., *South and Meso-American Native Spirituality: From the Cult of the Feathered Serpent to the Theology of Liberation* (New York, NY: The Crossroad Publishing Company, 1997), 41-64.

124. Davíd Carrasco, *Religions of Mesoamerica: Cosmovision and Ceremonial Centers* (Long Grove, IL: Waveland Press, 1990), 24-56. Carrasco defines "cosmovision" as "the ways in which Mesoamericans *combined their cosmological notions relating to time and space into a structured and systematic worldview*" (*Religions of Mesoamerica,* xvii, italics in original).

125. León-Portilla, "Those Made Worthy," 42; Carrasco, *Religions,* 45-48.

126. León-Portilla, "Those Made Worthy," 41. León-Portilla quotes Bernal Díaz, among the first Spaniards to chronicle the Mesoamerican landscape: "[t]here were so many diabolical things...and many hearts of Indians...and everything was so clotted by blood, and there was so much of it, that I curse the whole of it."

127. Carrasco, *Religions,* 91: "...some impersonators [of the god Tezcatlipoca] surrendered willingly, even with courageous displays of devotion to the sacrificial destiny."

128. Ibid., 79-81.

129. Ibid., 80.

130. Elizondo, *La Morenita,* 15, 60-62.

131. Ibid., 103.

132. Miguel León-Portilla, ed., *Native Mesoamerican Spirituality: Ancient Myths, Discourses, Stories, Doctrines, Hymns, Poems from the Aztec, Yucatec, Quiche-Maya and Other Sacred Traditions* (Mahwah, NJ: Paulist Press, 1980), 47-49, 241-253.

133. Ibid., 244.

134. Tavard, *Beauty*; González, *Beauty and Justice*..

135. Tavard, *Beauty,* 188.

136. González, *Beauty and Justice.* González' theoretical understanding of a "theology of beauty" is interspersed throughout her book, but analyzed most thoroughly from a historical perspective in pages 153-183.

137. Among many who have seen the *Sueño* as "a poem of knowledge," see especially Octavio Paz, "Foreword," in *A Sor Juana Anthology,* trans. Alan S. Trueblood (Cambridge, MA: Harvard University Press, 1988), ix.

138. Elizondo, *La Morenita,* 14. Elizondo has a very positive attitude toward *flor y canto* and yet seems to acknowledge its fundamentally intuitive nature and the related issue of verifiability.

139. A helpful overview of a number of readings of Sor Juana's silence is by Geoff Guevara-Geer, "The Final Silence of Sor Juana: The Abysmal Remove of Her Closing Night," in Bergmann and Schlau, eds., *Approaches,* 201-208.

140. Roberto S. Goizueta, "U.S. Hispanic Popular Catholicism as Theopoetics." In *Hispanic/Latino Theology: Challenge and Promise,* Ada María Isasi-Díaz and Fernando Segovia, eds. (Minneapolis: Fortress Press, 1996), 261-288.

141. Goizueta, "Theopoetics," 261.
142. Goizueta, "Theopoetics," 261.
143. Ibid., 262.
144. Goizueta, "Theopoetics," 263.
145. Goizueta, "Theopoetics," 262. Italics mine.
146. Goizueta, "Theopoetics," 265.
147. Ibid., 266.
148. Lindbeck, *Nature*.
149. Lindbeck, *Nature,* 35.
150. Ibid., 36.
151. Peden, *Poems,* 229, 237.
152. Goizueta, "Theopoetics," 286.
153. Goizueta, "Theopoetics," 286.
154. Margaret Sayers Peden, *Poems, Protest, and a Dream* (New York, New York: Penguin Books), 125.
155. Rappaport, *Selected Writings,* 69-88.
156. Ibid., 17.
157. The references to the *Loa* throughout this summary depend on the translation by Margaret Sayers Peden in *Sor Juana Inés de la Cruz: Poems, Protest, and a Dream*, 194-239.
158. Rappaport, *Selected Writings*, 69.
159. Rappaport, *Selected Writings*, 88.
160. A helpful chart outlining the basic differences between these epistemologies is included in Elizondo, *La Morenita,* 60-62.
161. Elias L. Rivers, "Sor Juana's *Dream:* In Search of a Scientific Vision," in Bergmann and Schlau, eds., *Approaches*, 128.
162. Current Spanish usage prefers "primer" over "primero," a fact which leads to some ambiguity in translation. A brief discussion of this subject as it pertains to the *Sueño* is included in Peden, *Poems,* vi-vii.
163. Tavard, *Beauty,* 14.
164. Rivers, *Dream*, 127.
165. Rappaport, *Selected Writings*, 286.
166. Tavard, *Beauty*, 15.
167. Rivers, "Sor Juana's *Dream,*" in Bergmann and Schlau, eds., *Approaches,* 127.
168. Ibid., 127-128.
169. [18] Paz, *Traps,* 380.
170. The following synopsis relies on the facing-pages bilingual version edited and translated by Peden, *Poems,* 79-129.

171. Paz, *Traps*, 377.
172. Paz, *Traps*, 177.
173. Paz, *Traps*, 377.
174. David Jasper, *Rhetoric, Power and Community: An Exercise in Reserve* (Louisville, KY: Westminster/John Knox Press, 1993)., 38. Italics mine.
175. Rappaport, *Selected Writings*, 20.
176. Eseamilla-Elizalde, "La 'Respuesta,'" 6.
177. Rappaport, *Selected Writings,* 221; Eseamilla-Elizalde, "La 'Respuesta,'" 6.
178. Ibid., 253.
179. Eseamilla-Elizalde, "La 'Respuesta,'" 2-5.
180. Rappaport, *Selected Writings*, 289.
181. Ibid., 250-251.
182. Ibid., 254.
183. Ibid., 256.
184. Octavio Paz, *Sor Juana Inés de la Cruz o las trampas de la fe.* Barcelona: Editorial Seix Barral, S. A., 1982, 16.
185. Paz, *Trampas,* 16.
186. Ibid., 17.
187. Paz, *Trampas*, 17, paraphrase and emphasis are mine.
188. Jasper, *Rhetoric*, x.
189. Ibid., x-xi.
190. Jasper, *Rhetoric,* 94. Italics mine.
191. Some readers of Sor Juana—but certainly not all—believe that her literary silence after the *Respuesta* was a direct result of the admonitions of the Bishop. Various interpretations of Sor Juana's silence are summarized by Rappaport, *Selected Writings,* 22-24; as well as Guevara-Geer, "The Final Silence of Sor Juana," in Bergmann and Schlau, eds., *Approaches,* 201-208.
192. Rappaport, *Selected Writings,* 255.
193. Ibid., 255.
194. Paz, *Trampas*, 16.
195. Paz, *Traps*, 397.
196. Ibid.
197. Sor Juana Inés de la Cruz, *Works,* 37. Paraphrase mine.
198. Rappaport, *Selected Writings*, 286.
199. Paz, *Traps,* 278.
200. Ibid., 277.

201. Georges Bataille, *Theory of Religion,* Robert Hurley, trans. (New York: Zone Books, 1989), 50.

202. Ibid., 52.

203. http://www.prosopagnosiaresearch.org/index/information.

204. From the "Respuesta," Margaret Sayers Peden, Poems, Protest, and a Dream (New York, New York: Penguin Books, 1997), 41.

205. Frederick Buechner, Wishful Thinking: A Seeker's ABC (San Francisco: Harper San Francisco, 1993).

206. Peden, Poems, 45.

207. Grady C. Wray, "Sacred Allusions: Theology in Sor Juana's Work," in Bergmann and Schlau, eds., Approaches, 71.

208. Margaret Sayers Peden, Poems, Protest, and a Dream (New York, New York: Penguin Books, 1997), 13.

209. Ibid., 15.

210. Ibid.

211. Ibid.

212. Peden, Poems, 15.

213. Ibid.,15-16.

214. Ibid., 17.

215. Peden, Poems, 17, emphasis in original.

216. Ibid.

217. Ibid., 19.

218. Peden, Poems, 25.

219. Ibid.

220. Ibid., 39.

221. Ibid., emphasis in original.

222. Ibid., 43.

223. Ibid., 42, my paraphrase.

224. Ibid., 45.

225. Ibid., 137; 140-141.

226. Yolanda Martínez-San Miguel, "Response to Michelle González," 26-30.

227. Mary Wollstonecraft and Candace Ward, A Vindication of the Rights of Woman (Mineola, NY: Dover Publications, 1996).

228. See especially the work of Jean-Jacques Rousseau, whose novel Emile is often seen as an indication of increased interest in the individual self as a category for analyzing rights and responsibilities for citizenship. Rousseau, Jean-Jacques. Emile: Or, On Education (New York: Basic Books, 1979).

229. Virginia Woolf, A Room of One's Own (Mansfield Centre, CN: Martino Publishing, 2012).

230. González, Justice, 93.

231. Ibid., in reference to the work of José González Boixo.

232. Ibid., 94.

233. Ibid.

234. Rappaport, Selected Writings, 1.

235. Whether or not Paul actually wrote the letter to Timothy in which this passage appears was not an active question during Sor Juana's time.

236. Paz, Traps, 459.

237. Nina M. Scott, "Sor Juana Inés de la Cruz: Three Hundred Years of Controversy and Counting," in Bergmann and Schlau, eds., Approaches, 193-200.

238. Peden, Poems, 59.

239. Anna Karin Hammar, "After Forty Years: Churches in Solidarity with Women?" Ecumenical Review 40, no. 3-4 (July 1, 1988): 528-538.

240. Ibid., 531.

241. Irja Askola, "Turning Means Returning: The Assembly Theme and Churches' Solidarity with Women." Ecumenical Review 50, no. 2 (April 1998): 190-195.

242. Ibid., 191.

243. Ibid., 193.

244. Ibid., 193.

245. Ibid., 193-194.

246. Octavio Paz, *Sor Juana: Or, the Traps of Faith*, trans. Margaret Sayers Peden (Cambridge, MA: The Belknap Press of Harvard University Press, 1988), 146.